WITTGENSTEIN'S CONCEPTION OF PHILOSOPHY

Wittgenstein's Conception of Philosophy

K. T. Fann

UNIVERSITY OF CALIFORNIA PRESS
Berkeley and Los Angeles 1971

University of California Press
Berkeley and Los Angeles, California

© Basil Blackwell 1969

Library of Congress Catalog Card Number: 72–89890

First California Paperbound Printing 1971

(with enlarged Selected Addenda to Bibliography)

ISBN: 0–520–01837–0

Printed in the United States of America

Our misapprehension of the nature of language has occasioned a greater waste of time, and effort, and genius, than all the other mistakes and delusions with which humanity has been afflicted. It has retarded immeasurably our physical knowledge of every kind, and vitiated what it could not retard. The misapprehension exists still in unmitigated virulence; and though metaphysicks, a rank branch of the errour, is fallen into disrepute, it is abandoned like a mine which will not repay the expense of working, rather than like a process of mining which we have discovered to be constitutionally incapable of producing gold.

Alexander Bryan Johnson: *A Treatise on Language*, 1836

For

SANDRA LEE

Contents

Abbreviations

Abbreviations used in referring to the following editions of Wittgenstein's writings. Departures from the standard translations are indicated in the footnotes.

T. *Tractatus Logico-Philosophicus*. Translated by D. F. Pears and B. F. McGuinness (London, 1961).

Nb. *Notebooks 1914–16*. Translated by G. E. M. Anscombe (Oxford, 1961).

P.B. *Philosophische Bemerkungen*. German version only (Oxford, 1965).

B.B. *Blue and Brown Books*. Oxford, 1958.

P.I. *Philosophical Investigations*. Translated by G. E. M. Anscombe (Oxford, 1958).

R.F.M. *Remarks on the Foundations of Mathematics*. Translated by G. E. M. Anscombe (Oxford, 1956).

Z. *Zettel*. Translated by G. E. M. Anscombe (Oxford, 1967).

Preface

It is a peculiarity of philosophical activity that the investigation of the nature, tasks and methods of philosophy constitutes a most important part of the whole enterprise. Every 'revolution' in philosophy involves essentially a radical change in the conception of philosophy itself. If there has been a revolution in philosophy in recent years it is largely due to Wittgenstein's perceptions into the nature of philosophy. According to G. E. Moore, Wittgenstein claimed that what he was doing was a 'new' subject, and not merely a stage in a 'continuous development'; that there was now, in philosophy, a 'kink' in the development of human thought comparable to that which occurred when Galileo and his contemporaries invented dynamics; that a 'new method' had been found, as had happened when chemistry was developed out of alchemy.[1]

How is this 'new subject' related to traditional philosophy and why should it be called 'philosophy'? In answering, Wittgenstein said that though what he was doing was certainly different from what traditional philosophers had done, yet people might be inclined to say 'This is what I really wanted' and to identify it with what they had done, just as a person who had been trying to trisect an angle by rule and compasses might, when shown the proof that this is impossible, be inclined to say that this impossible thing was the very thing he had been trying to do,

[1] G. E. Moore, 'Wittgenstein's Lectures in 1930–33', in his *Philosophical Papers* (London, 1959), p. 322.

though what he had been trying to do was really different.[1]

This analogy is quite appropriate and illuminating. If traditional philosophy is characterized as different attempts at answering various philosophical questions then Wittgenstein's philosophy may be characterized as a systematic questioning of the questions themselves. He was reported to have said that he didn't *solve* philosophical problems but *dissolved* them. This is clearly shown by his statement: 'For the clarity we are aiming at is indeed *complete* clarity. But this simply means that the philosophical problems should *completely* disappear' (P.I. §133).

Wittgenstein's intellectual life is divided much more definitely than most into two distinct major periods. The first is represented by *Tractatus Logico-Philosophicus*, and the second by *Philosophical Investigations*. It is my aim here to seek a clear understanding of Wittgenstein's conception of philosophy by comparing and contrasting his earlier and later views. Wittgenstein himself wished to publish the *Tractatus* and the *Investigations* together because, as he puts it, ' . . . the latter could be seen in the right light only by contrast with and against the background of my old way of thinking. For since beginning to occupy myself with philosophy again . . ., I have been forced to recognize grave mistakes in what I wrote in that first book' (P.I. p. x).

The relation between the *Tractatus* and the *Investigations* is a matter of controversy. On the one hand, the passage just quoted has been interpreted to mean that 'Wittgenstein himself viewed . . . [the *Investigations*] as a development or deepening of [the *Tractatus*], and in fact, . . . both the one and the other only makes sense when they are seen as complementary.'[2] On the other hand, the majority of commentators seem to agree with Hartnack in maintaining that 'No unbroken line leads from the *Tractatus* to the *Philoso-*

---

[1] Ibid., p. 323.
[2] M. J. Charlesworth, *Philosophy and Linguistic Analysis* (Pittsburgh, 1961), p. 76.

phical Investigations; there is no logical sequence between the two books, but rather a logical gap. The thought of the later work is a negation of the thought of the earlier.'[1]

One asserts that the *Investigations*, as a whole, is a 'development' of the *Tractatus* while the other claims that they are 'negations' of each other. Both interpretations are radically mistaken. Wittgenstein himself used to say that the *Tractatus* was not *all* wrong: it was not like a bag of junk professing to be a clock, but like a clock that did not tell you the right time.[2] It is important to distinguish clearly the part of the *Tractatus* which was repudiated from the part which was not. Wittgenstein merely advises us to contrast his later work with his old *way* of thinking—i.e. his old method of philosophizing. It is quite true that his new and old *ways* of thinking are poles apart. The *Tractatus* follows the methods of traditional theoretic construction (even though to construct only a 'ladder' to be abandoned at the end) while the *Investigations* employs what can best be described as the method of dialectic. However, there is an important continuity in Wittgenstein's conception of the nature and tasks of philosophy. The views arrived at in the *Tractatus* (that philosophical problems arise from our misunderstanding of the logic of our language, that philosophy is no science but an activity of elucidation and clarification, etc.) continued to serve as the leading thread in Wittgenstein's later works. Thus, Wittgenstein's later *conception* of the nature and tasks of philosophy can best be seen as a 'development' of his earlier views, while his later *method* should be regarded as the 'negation' of his earlier method. This, I think, is the key to a clear understanding of Wittgenstein's philosophy as a whole.

The method of my presentation is, therefore, to give an exposition and 'interpretation' of the *Tractatus* first (in Part 1) and then (in Part 2) to bring out the sharp contrast between his earlier and later views before his later conception

[1] J. Hartnack, *Wittgenstein and Modern Philosophy* (London, 1965), p. 49.
[2] G. E. M. Anscombe, *An Introduction to Tractatus* (London, 1959), p. 78.

of philosophy is described in detail. I rely and concentrate mainly on the two texts cited. However, many other
published writings and a number of unpublished manu-
scripts and lecture notes are consulted.[1] A comprehensive
bibliography is given at the end of this book.

This book is intended as a brief introduction to Wittgenstein's works for students and the interested public. It is the
result of my own struggle to understand Wittgenstein and
was originally written in 1966–7 as my doctoral dissertation
at the University of Hawaii. The guide-line of my interpretation is to take Wittgenstein's words at their face value.
However, I have read and benefited greatly from many
writings about Wittgenstein. Unfortunately, I am unable
to give all credits where they are due. I would like to express my gratitude to my friend and former teacher, Richard
P. Haynes, with whom I have had many valuable philosophical discussions. Special thanks are due to the publishers and their anonymous readers of my manuscript who
have made a number of helpful comments.

[1] Since the completion of the manuscript two more important source
materials have appeared: *Wittgenstein und der Wiener Kreis* (shorthand
notes recorded by F. Waismann) and *Letters from Wittgenstein with a
Memoir* (by Paul Engelmann). However these materials have not been
incorporated into the finished text, as they do not alter my main con-
tentions.

PART 1

The Early Wittgenstein

Half of what I say is meaningless. I say it so that the other half may reach you.

Kahlil Gibran

My work consists of two parts: the one presented here plus all that I have *not* written. And it is precisely this second part that is the important one.

Ludwig Wittgenstein

CHAPTER I

Preliminary

Wittgenstein's early philosophy is represented by the *Tractatus* which he completed before he was thirty years old. It consists of short oracular remarks characterized by a striking combination of logical precision and poetic vagueness. Within a span of some 80 pages the whole range of philosophy is dealt with. There are comments on the nature of the world, the essence of language, the nature of logic and mathematics and insights about the nature of philosophy, not to mention interesting remarks about the philosophy of science, ethics, religion and mysticism.

Because of the difficulty of the subject matter and the cryptic style of presentation, the *Tractatus* is without doubt one of the hardest philosophic classics to master.[1] Wittgenstein says in the Preface, 'Perhaps this book will be understood only by someone who has himself already had the thoughts that are expressed in it—or at least similar thoughts.' He told Frank Ramsey that his idea of the work was 'not that anyone by reading it will understand his ideas but that some day someone will think them out again for

[1] The *Tractatus* has been compared to many Western classics, but the one classic it resembles most is the Old Master's *Tao Teh Ching*. Both are composed of short oracular remarks which cover the whole range of philosophy in a short span. Both philosophers use paradoxes to convey their most important insights. One starts with a metaphysical statement about the nature of the world and ends with the practical advice: Whereof one cannot speak one must be silent; while the other starts with a metaphysical statement about the Way of Nature and concludes with a practical message: Do nothing and nothing will be left undone.

himself and will derive great pleasure from finding in his book their exact expression.'[1] According to Wittgenstein himself, it was misunderstood by Russell, Moore and Frege—the three foremost philosphers of his time.[2]

Although the *Tractatus* remains difficult and open to various interpretations, it is no longer as forbidding as it was when it first appeared. Now we are in a better position to appreciate the problems Wittgenstein was dealing with. Our understanding is greatly helped by the publication of 'Notes on Logic' prepared for Russell in 1913, the 'Notes' dictated to Moore in 1914, the letters to Russell written in that period, and especially the *Notebooks* from which Wittgenstein extracted much of the final text. Also helpful are Wittgenstein's later works in which the *Tractatus* is criticized. My treatment of the *Tractatus* is necessarily sketchy as I am mainly interested in his conception and method of philosophy.

What is the *Tractatus* all about? The keynote is struck in the Preface where Wittgenstein says: 'The books deal with

[1] From Ramsey's letter to his mother written on September 10th, 1923 while visiting Wittgenstein. Included in F. A. von Hayek's *Biographical Sketch of Wittgenstein* (unpublished).

[2] From a prison camp in Italy he wrote in April, 1919 to Russell about the completed manuscript: 'I believe that I've solved our problems finally. This may sound arrogant but I can't help believing it.' But he adds, 'you would not understand it without a previous explanation as it's written in quite short remarks'. On August 19th of the same year, he wrote to Russell again and mentioned, 'I also sent my MS. to Frege. He wrote me a week ago and I gather that he doesn't understand a word of it at all. So my only hope is to see you soon and to explain all to you, . . .'. But after explaining the *Tractatus* 'line by line' (according to Russell), Wittgenstein declined to have Russell's introduction printed with his work. He wrote: 'Your introduction will not be printed, and in consequence probably neither will my book. For when I got the German translation of the introduction, I couldn't bring myself to have it printed with my work after all. For the fineness of your English style was—of course—quite lost and what was left was superficiality and misunderstanding.' The above quotations are from von Hayek's unpublished *Biographical Sketch* except the last which is reprinted in Nb. p. 131.

the problems of philosophy, and shows, I believe, that the reason why these questions are posed is that the logic of our language is misunderstood.' The implication is that the problems should not even be posed if the logic of our language is correctly understood. This sums up both the aim and the method of the book. To put it paradoxically: the whole aim of his philosophizing in the *Tractatus* is to put an end to philosophizing. Wittgenstein will achieve this by setting a limit to thought, or rather to the expression of thoughts—i.e. language. 'It will therefore only be in language that the limit can be set, and what lies on the other side of the limit will be simply nonsense' (Preface, p. 3). Thus, the principal job of the *Tractatus* is to investigate the essence of language—its function and its structure (cf. P.I. §92).

Before turning to Wittgenstein's account of the nature of language we should first look at the basic assumptions which lie behind the method of the *Tractatus*. Wittgenstein assumes that the structure of language is revealed by logic and that the essential function of language is to depict or to describe the world. Thus, there are two major questions to be answered: (1) What is the nature of logic? and (2) How is language related to the world?

Logic, Language and the World. These are the three master-issues of the *Tractatus*. In 'Notes on Logic' Wittgenstein wrote, 'Philosophy consists of logic and metaphysics, the former its basis' (Nb. p. 93). Why did he think that logic was the basis of metaphysics? No explanation was offered in the *Tractatus* except the assertion: 'Logic is . . . a mirror-image of the world' (T. 6.13). However, an explanation is contained in the *Investigations*, where he severely criticized the basic assumptions of the *Tractatus*. 'For there seemed to pertain to logic a peculiar depth—a universal significance. Logic lay, it seemed, at the bottom of all sciences.—For logical investigation explores the nature of all things' (P.I. §89). And, 'Thought is surrounded by a halo.—Its essence, logic, presents an order, in fact the a priori order of the world: that is, the order of *possibilities*, which must be common to both world and thought' (P.I. §97).

It should be kept in mind while studying Wittgenstein's early writings that his study of logic and language always had ontological implications. 'The great problem round which everything that I write turns is: Is there an order in the world *a priori*, and if so what does it consist in?' (Nb. p. 53). He was preoccupied with the perennial problem of the connection between thought or language, and the world. That there must be 'an *a priori* order in the world' was a conviction the young Wittgenstein never questioned ('The world has a fixed structure', Nb. p. 62). The reasoning behind Wittgenstein's method probably ran as follows: For us to think and talk about the world there must be something common between language and the world. The common element must lie in their structures. We can know the structure of one if we know the structure of the other. Since logic reveals the structure of language it must also reveal the structure of the world. It is quite clear that Wittgenstein's order of investigation is thus: from the nature of logic to the nature of language and then to the nature of the world.[1] This is confirmed by an entry in his *Notebooks*: 'My work has extended from the foundations of logic to the nature of the world' (Nb, p. 79).

This order of investigation, however, is roughly the reverse of the order of presentation in the finished text. In the *Tractatus* Wittgenstein starts with the propositions: 'The world is all that is the case' (T. 1.0). 'The world is the totality of facts, not of things' (T. 1.1). Though these statements

---

[1] This was roughly Frege's and Russell's procedure also. Russell set himself the problem of determining 'Whether anything, and if so, what, can be inferred from the structure of language as to the structure of the world'. *Inquiry into Meaning and Truth* (London, 1940), p. 429. Cf. G. H. von Wright, 'Biographical Sketch' in K. T. Fann (ed.): *Ludwig Wittgenstein: The Man and His Philosophy* (New York, 1967), p. 17.

stand at the beginning, they are best regarded as conclusions from what follows. The account of the nature of the world is given first because it anticipates and is required by the theory of language which comes later. The meaning of these metaphysical statements cannot be fully appreciated until his account of the nature of language is understood.

CHAPTER II

Language

Briefly stated, Wittgenstein's theory of language in the *Tractatus* has two components: the 'picture theory' and the 'truth-function theory'. These two theories are designed to answer the questions: 'What is the function of language?' and 'What is the structure of language?' Since language is conceived as 'the totality of propositions' (T. 4.001), the two questions are transformed into the following: 'How are propositions related to the world?' and 'How are propositions related to one another?' This is why Wittgenstein wrote in his *Notebook*, 'My *whole* task consists in explaining the nature of the proposition' (Nb. p. 39). Wittgenstein assumes that if we can use language to talk about the world there must be some propositions directly connected with the world, so that their truth or falsity are not determined by other propositions but by the world: these he called 'elementary propositions'. Non-elementary propositions are understood *via* elementary ones; their truth or falsity are determined by (or are functions of) the elementary propositions. Accordingly the two questions above now take the following forms: 'How are elementary propositions linked with the world?' and 'How are complex propositions related to elementary ones?' His answers are: Elementary propositions are 'logical pictures' of atomic facts—the basic kind of facts which cannot be further analysed; and all complex propositions are 'truth-functions' of the elementary ones.

To understand Wittgenstein's solution it is important to realize that his method of analysis was necessitated *a priori*.

As he later pointed out, ' . . . the crystalline purity of logic
was, of course, not a *result of investigation*: it was a requirement' (P.I. §107). He was convinced that language must
have such and such features in order for a connection with
the world to be possible. In other words, he was looking for
the *a priori* conditions for language to *work*.

Paraphrasing Kant's question about the synthetic *a priori*,
Wittgenstein's question is: '*How* is it possible to make statements about the world?' The fact is that language *is* possible,
it is possible to make statements about the world; what he
wants to know is: '*How* is it possible?' It would be quite wrong
to suppose that Wittgenstein is concerned with constructing
a 'logically perfect language' as Russell assumes in his Introduction to the *Tractatus*. Wittgenstein makes it quite clear that,
' . . . all the propositions of our everyday language, just as
they stand, are in perfect logical order' (T. 5.5563). In fact he
states in his *Notebook*, 'I only want to justify the vagueness of
ordinary propositions; for it *can* be justified' (Nb. p. 70). This,
let it be noted, is also the aim of the *Investigations*; although the
method of justifying ordinary language in it is quite different.
In the *Tractatus* Wittgenstein employs the purely *a priori*
method to show that vague propositions are really not vague
at all once their logical structures are revealed by analysis.
He says in the *Investigations*, 'We ask: "*What is* language?"
"*What is* a proposition?" And the answer to these questions
is to be given once for all; and independently of any future
experience' (P.I. §92). It is precisely in this *a priori* search for
the once-for-all solutions to philosophical problems that the
Tractatus contrasts most sharply with the *Investigations*.

The *a priori* character of Wittgenstein's method is most
clearly manifested in the way he arrived at the notions of
elementary proposition and atomic fact.[1] An elementary

---

[1] 'Sachverhalt' has been variously translated as 'state of affairs',
situation', or 'prime fact'. Nevertheless 'atomic fact' is most appropriate as 'Sachverhalt' denotes a kind of fact which cannot be analysed
further and Wittgenstein himself acccepted this translation.

proposition is simply one that cannot be analysed into any further, more basic propositions. All ordinary propositions are complex, they can be analysed into other, simpler propositions; and these, in turn, could be further analysed into a class of absolutely basic propositions of which no such further analysis is possible—these are the elementary propositions.

It would be interesting to retrace the steps (contained in his *Notebooks*) from which Wittgenstein arrived at elementary propositions. It is clear, Wittgenstein points out in the *Notebooks*, that the propositions we use in daily life ' . . . have a sense just as they are and do not wait upon a future analysis in order to acquire a sense' (Nb. p. 62) and that the person who asserts something *knows* what he *means* by the vague proposition. But someone else may not understand and ask: 'What do you mean by *this* and *that* term?'; and someone else again will not understand the explanation and will demand further explanation (Nb. p. 70). For example, if I assert, 'Wittgenstein is a philosopher', I know what I mean. But someone may ask 'Who is Wittgenstein and what is a philosopher?' I can try to describe Wittgenstein and define 'philosopher', but terms in my description and definition may in turn be open to question. This process of *analysis* may go on indefinitely but if it is true that we can make statements about the world then the process must some time come to an end (Nb. p. 46), and the end product must, somehow, be in direct contact with the world.

What does the end product of analysis—the elementary proposition—look like? Wittgenstein wrote in his *Notebooks*, 'In all the propositions that occur to me there occur names, which, however, must disappear on further analysis. I know that such a further analysis is possible, but am unable to carry it out completely. In spite of this I certainly seem to know that if the analysis were completely carried out, its result would have to be a proposition which once more contained names, relations, etc. In brief, it looks as if in this way I know a form without being acquainted with any single example of it. I see that the analysis can be carried farther, and can, so to speak, not imagine its leading to anything different from the species of propositions that I am familiar with' (Nb. p. 61). Thus, although he was not able to carry out *in practice* a complete analysis and give examples of elementary propositions, he was sure, *a priori*, that there must be elementary propositions and what they must be like. In the *Tractatus* Wittgenstein writes: 'The *application* of logic decides what elementary propositions there are. What belongs to its application, logic cannot anticipate' (T. 5.557). The actual process of analysis belongs to the application of logic, it is an empirical matter which is of no concern to Wittgenstein's 'logical' investigation.

The *a priori* nature of Wittgenstein's method is clearly indicated in his conclusions about 'elementary propositions': 'If we know on purely logical grounds that there must be elementary propositions, then everyone who understands propositions in their unanalysed form must know it' (T. 5.5562). 'It is obvious that the analysis of propositions must bring us to elementary propositions which consist of names in immediate combination' (T. 4.221). 'An elementary proposition consists of names. It is a nexus, a concatenation, of names' (T. 4.22).

We are now in a strange position: On the one hand, 'elementary propositions' cannot be 'anything different from the species of propositions that I am familiar with'— i.e. 'a concatenation of names'; on the other hand, the names that occur in ordinary propositions 'must disappear on further analysis'. What are 'names' which are the constituents of elementary propositions?

Ordinary names such as 'Dog', 'Circle', and 'Plato' do not qualify as 'names' in the special sense Wittgenstein is using it, since they can be further analysed. 'A name cannot be dissected any further by means of a definition: it is a primitive sign' (T. 3.26). It follows from this that a name must refer to something simple—something without parts. If a name referred to something complex, it could be defined in terms of its constituents, and hence would not be a name. And if a term in a proposition refers to a complex then the proposition, by definition, cannot be 'elementary'.

That which a name refers to is called an 'object'. 'A name refers to an object' (T. 3.203). 'Objects are simple' (T. 2.02). Wittgenstein's line of reasoning is brought out very clearly in the following entry in his *Notebooks*: 'It seems that the idea of the SIMPLE is already to be found contained in that of the complex and in the idea of analysis, and in such a way that we come to this idea quite apart from any examples of simple objects, or of propositions which mention them, and we realize the existence of the simple object—*a priori*—as a logical necessity' (Nb. p. 60).

It is amazing that nowhere in all of Wittgenstein's writings are we offered a single example of 'names' or 'elementary propositions'. Malcolm reports: 'I asked Wittgenstein whether, when he wrote the *Tractatus*, he had ever decided upon anything as an *example* of a 'simple object'. His reply was that at that time his thought had been that he was a *logician*; and that it was not his business, as a logician, to try to decide whether this thing or that was a simple thing or a complex thing, that being a purely *empirical* matter! It was clear that he regarded his former opinion as absurd.'[1] In all fairness to Wittgenstein, however, he was not completely blind to the difficulty. Expressions of doubt were contained in his 1915 entries such as: 'Our difficulty was that we kept on speaking of simple objects and were unable to mention a single one' (Nb. p. 68); and, '*Is it*, A PRIORI, *clear that in analysing we must arrive at simple components—is this, e.g., involved in the concept of analysis—*, or is analysis *ad infinitum* possible?—Or is there in the end even a third possibility?' (Nb. p. 62).

These doubts were either overcome or suppressed by the

[1] N. Malcolm: *Ludwig Wittgenstein: A Memoir* (London, 1958), p. 86.

time the *Tractatus* was composed. At any rate, in the *Tractatus* Wittgenstein contends that any ordinary propositions (no matter how vague) can be analysed into a set of elementary propositions which consist of nothing but simple terms (or names). He concludes, furthermore, that there must be simple things—i.e., objects—which correspond to the names. He shares the assumption of traditional philosophers that the meaning of a name is the object it denotes. 'A name refers to an object. The object is its reference' (T. 3.203).[1] If objects do not exist, the elementary propositions would consist of terms without reference and would thus be senseless. But since the sense of all propositions depends ultimately on that of the elementary ones, no proposition would have any sense, which is patently false. Hence, there must be objects.

It would be worthwhile to quote at length what Wittgenstein says in the *Investigations* about his reasoning behind the notion of 'name' and 'object' in the *Tractatus*: 'The word "Excalibur", say, is a proper name in the ordinary sense. The sword Excalibur consists of parts combined in a particular way. If they are combined differently Excalibur does not exist. But it is clear that the sentence "Excalibur has a sharp blade" makes *sense* whether Excalibur is still whole or is broken up. But if "Excalibur" is the name of an object, this object no longer exists when Excalibur is broken in pieces; and as no object would then correspond to the name it would have no meaning. But then the sentence "Excalibur has a sharp blade" would contain a word that had no meaning, and hence the sentence would be nonsense. But it does make sense; so there must always be something

---

[1] Wittgenstein adopted the distinction between 'Sinn' (sense) and 'Bedeutung' (reference) from Frege. However, while Frege made the distinction with regard to sentences, Wittgenstein contends that sentences can only have *Sinn* and words (or names) have *Bedeutung*. I shall stick to Wittgenstein's distinction and translate 'Bedeutung' as 'reference' and 'bedeuten' as 'to refer'.

corresponding to the words of which it consists. So the word "Excalibur" must disappear when the sense is analysed and its place be taken by words which name simples' (P.I. §39). Again: ' "A *name* signifies only what is an *element* of reality. What cannot be destroyed; what remains the same in all changes." . . . We say that the back is part of the chair, but is in turn itself composed of several bits of wood; while a leg is a single component part. We also see a whole which changes (is destroyed) while its component parts remain unchanged. These are the materials from which we construct that picture of reality' (P.I. §59)—Presumably the picture of reality contained in the *Tractatus*.

Thus, by a purely *a priori* consideration of language, Wittgenstein has arrived at an ontology: 'Objects make up the substance of the world' (T. 2.021), 'Empirical reality is limited by the totality of objects' (T. 5.5561). It would not be difficult now to see how the world is structured: it is made up of objects which hang together in a determinate way to form 'atomic facts', which in turn, make up 'facts' of whatever complexity. It is obvious that each of these, object, atomic fact, and fact, has its linguistic counterpart: name, elementary proposition, and proposition.

'The configuration of objects produces atomic facts' (T. 2.0272). 'In an atomic fact objects fit into one another like the links of a chain' (T. 2.03). The linguistic counterpart of the atomic fact—the elementary proposition 'asserts the existence of an atomic fact' (T. 4.21). To assert the existence of the atomic fact is to describe the configuration of objects. Hence, the general form of propositions is: '*This* is how things are.' 'If an elementary proposition is true, the atomic fact exists: if an elementary proposition is false, the atomic fact does not exist' (T. 4.25). But an elementary proposition is a concatenation of names. How can a list of names *say* anything? There are other puzzling features of language connected with propositions. How can we understand the sense of a proposition even if it is false or if it describes a non-existing entity?—e.g. 'Hawaii is the largest state in the Union' or 'The present king of France is bald.' Furthermore, how can a person understand a proposition which he has never run across before? All these questions boil down to one question, 'How are elementary propositions *possible*?' The answer is: 'It is a picture of the atomic fact.'

'In the proposition a world is as it were put together experimentally' (Nb. p. 7). This idea apparently occurred to him in a Paris traffic-court where he saw a traffic accident reconstructed by means of dolls and toys (ibid).[1] The important thing is that the *how* of the accident, the way the original participants were related at the time of the accident, is shown by the arrangement of dolls and toys which stand as *proxies* for the pedestrians, etc. 'A proposition is a model of reality as we imagine it' (T. 4.01). Similarly a picture represents or misrepresents a situation by virtue of the arrangement of dots, lines and colour patches on a paper. 'In a picture the elements of the picture are the representatives of objects' (T. 2.131).

How is a picture possible? 'What constitutes a picture is that its elements are related to one another in a determinate way' (T. 2.14). 'The fact that the elements of a picture are related to one another in a determinate way represents that things are related to one another in the same way' (T. 2.15). A picture of a situation, say X, *is a* picture of X and not Y because the way the elements of the picture are related—the *form* of the picture, is the same as the way the elements of X are related—the *form* of X. As Wittgenstein puts it, the logical structure of the picture and the situation pictured is identical. This identity makes it possible for the two-dimensional picture to depict reality which has more than two dimensions.

---

[1] It is characteristic of the method of *Tractatus* that Wittgenstein exclaimed at this point, 'It must be possible to demonstrate everything essential [about the proposition] by considering this case.' This method he later calls the 'one-sided diet' which causes philosophical disease.

In the same way, 'What constitutes a propositional sign [the sentence] is that in it its elements (the words) stand in a determinate relation to one another' (T. 3.14). But for a proposition to be a proposition about a certain situation it must have ' . . . exactly as many distinguishable parts as in the situation that it represents' (T. 4.04), otherwise it would not be a proposition about *that* specific situation. This means there must be a one-to-one correspondence between the elements of a proposition and those of the situation it describes. This requirement, however, can only be met by elementary propositions which alone consist entirely of names, each referring directly to an object. An elementary proposition is not merely a medley of names.—(Just as a theme in music is not a medley of notes) (T. 3.141). What makes it a proposition is that names are arranged in a determinate way—it has a logical structure which is identical to the way the objects of an atomic fact are arranged. There is a general rule correlating the elements of a proposition with the elements of a fact. One can, as it were, draw lines between names of an elementary proposition and objects of the atomic fact which is pictured by the elementary proposition. *That* is how an elementary proposition is in touch with the world; 'it reaches right out to it' (T. 2.1511).

If an elementary proposition *matches* the atomic fact it describes, then it is true; otherwise, it is false. But a proposition need not be compared with reality to be understood, because it is a picture of reality: I know the situation that it represents by merely looking at the picture. That is also the reason why we can understand a completely new proposition such as: 'There are ten pink elephants flying over Hawaii.' In all likelihood nobody has ever come across this statement before. Nevertheless, we all know what it means because it sketches out a picture which can be compared with the reality. Like a picture, 'A proposition *shows* its sense. [It] *shows* how things stand *if* it is true' (T. 4.022). Hence, 'To understand a proposition means to know what is the case if it is true. (One can understand it, therefore, without knowing whether it is true)' (T. 4.024).

The other important feature of Wittgenstein's theory of language—the truth-function theory—should be briefly described here. We have seen that ordinary propositions can be clarified by analysis—their sense can be completely spelled out by means of elementary propositions. Language consists of propositions and propositions can be analysed into elementary propositions. Hence, 'Suppose that I am given *all* elementary propositions: then I can simply ask what propositions I can construct out of them. And there I have *all* propositions, and *that* fixes their limits' (T. 4.51). What, however, is the exact relationship between ordinary propositions and elementary propositions? Wittgenstein's answer is that all non-elementary propositions are truth-functional compounds of elementary propositions. 'A proposition is a truth-function of elementary propositions' (T. 5). This is one of the central theses of the *Tractatus*. A full appreciation of this thesis requires an understanding of truth-functional logic. It suffices for our purpose to point out merely that a compound proposition, compounded of the propositions $P_1, P_2, \ldots, P_n$, is a truth-functional compound of $P_1, P_2, \ldots, P_n$ if and only if its truth or falsity is uniquely determined by the truth or falsity (the truth-values) of $P_1, \ldots, P_n$. In other words the truth-value of a compound proposition is completely determined by the truth-values of its components—once the truth-values of its components are given, the truth-value of the compound proposition can be calculated. Wittgenstein claims that all propositions are related to elementary propositions truth-functionally.

An elementary proposition can be true or false depending on whether it matches up with the world or not. Given all elementary propositions, if we knew which were true and which false, the world would have been completely described, because the truth-value of any other proposition is entirely determined by the truth-values of its component elementary propositions (T. 4.26).

Wittgenstein does not offer clear reasons for thinking that all propositions are truth-functions of elementary ones. In the *Tractatus* we merely find different attempts to show that some apparent exceptions (such as 'attitude' propositions; universal propositions; and existential propositions)[1] are in fact truth-functions, some others (such as metaphysical propositions) are ruled out as not being genuine propositions at all (as nonsense), and still others (such as logical propositions), although propositions, are degenerate ones which say nothing.

Why must all genuine propositions be truth-functional? Anscombe writes, ' . . . The picture theory does not permit any functions of propositions other than truth-functions. Indeed, we should not regard Wittgenstein's theory of the proposition as *synthesis* of the picture theory and the theory of truth-function;[2] his picture theory and theory of truth-functions are one and the same.'[3] The important thing here is to realize that the truth-function theory is *demanded* by the picture theory. An elementary proposition says something in so far as it is a picture which can be compared with reality. It must be capable of being true or false depending on whether it corresponds to an atomic fact or not, it cannot be true (or false) *a priori*. As pointed out before, Wittgenstein thought that the end result of analysis (elementary propositions) must not be anything different from the species of propositions which are being analysed (Nb. p. 61). Since elementary propositions have sense in so far as they can be compared to reality, all propositions must be so accordingly; i.e. they must be capable of being true or

---

[1] The detailed treatment of these topics is irrelevant to the present thesis and hence will not be included.

[2] von Wright's contention. See: Fann (ed.) op. cit. p. 18.

[3] G. E. M. Anscombe, *An Introduction to Wittgenstein's Tractatus* (London, 1959), p. 81.

false. If a certain set of elementary propositions constitutes the complete analysis of a proposition, the truth-value of that proposition must be completely determined by the truth-values of those elementary propositions. In other words: all propositions are truth-functions of elementary propositions.

For example: if a proposition P_1 is completely analysed by two elementary propositions; p and q, and they are connected by the truth-functional connective 'and', then the truth-value of P_1 is completely determined by those of p and q in the following way:

p	q	P_1
T	T	T
T	F	F
F	T	F
F	F	F

That is to say, P_1 is true if p and q are both true, otherwise P_1 is false. P_1 is thus capable of being true or false, but whether it is true or false depends completely on the truth-values of its components. Hence P_1 qualifies as a genuine 'proposition'—it has 'sense'. Wittgenstein has shown that for any proposition, given its complete analysis in terms of elementary propositions, there is a mechanical method to test whether the proposition has 'sense' or not (T. 4.31, etc.).

Two extreme cases appear when the mechanical method (or what is now called 'truth-value analysis') is applied to propositions such as: P_2: 'It is raining or it is not', and P_3: 'It is raining and it is not.' If 'r' represents 'It is raining' and '−r' represents 'It is not raining' then we have the following situations:

r	−r	P_2	P_3
T	F	T	F
F	T	T	F

P_2 is true and P_3 is false regardless of the truth-values of r. In other words the truth-values of these propositions are not determined by those of their components—hence, by definition, they are without 'sense' or senseless. A proposition which is true for all truth-possibilities of the elementary propositions is called a *tautology* and a proposition which is false for all truth-possibilities is called a *contradiction* (T. 4.46). 'Propositions show what they say: tautologies and contradictions show that they say nothing. . . . (For example, I know nothing about the weather when I know that it is either raining or not raining.)' (T. 4.461). Any ordinary propositions which, when analysed, turn out to be tautologies or contradictions are not 'propositions' in the strict sense; they may be called 'degenerate' propositions. Any other ordinary propositions which, under scrutiny, turn out to be incapable of being subjected to truth-value analysis, are considered 'nonsense'; they are not propositions at all, but pseudo-propositions.

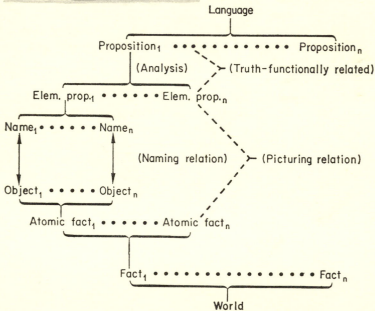

We have now a clear picture of Wittgenstein's view of language and the world. It is a neat system which can be diagrammatically represented, as shown opposite.

If the diagram is folded horizontally along the middle line, the terms in the upper half coincide perfectly with the terms in the lower half. Language is a mirror-image of the world.

Summarily then, language consists of propositions. All propositions can be analysed into elementary propositions and are truth-functions of elementary propositions. The elementary propositions are immediate combinations of names, which directly refer to objects; and elementary propositions are logical pictures of atomic facts, which are immediate combinations of objects. Atomic facts combine to form facts of whatever complexity which constitute the world. Thus language is truth-functionally structured and its essential function is to describe the world. Here we have the limit of language and what amounts to the same, the limit of the world.

CHAPTER III

What Cannot Be Said

According to the above theory, 'language' is identical to 'descriptive' language and to 'say' anything is equivalent to 'describing' something. Thus 'the totality of true propositions is the whole of natural science' (T. 4.11) and 'what can be said' is identified as 'propositions of natural science' (T. 6.53), or 'empirical propositions'. What about propositions of logic, mathematics, ethics, aesthetics, metaphysics, and so on? Wittgenstein devotes the remainder of the *Tractatus* to tracing out the consequences of his theory of language and concludes that propositions of logic, ethics, etc. do not say anything. They are senseless or nonsensical because they are attempts to transcend, in *language*, the limit of language and, hence, the world. Nevertheless, Wittgenstein contends that there are important things (moral and aesthetic values, meaning of life, etc.) which, although they cannot be *said*, can be *shown*. 'They are what is mystical' (T. 6.522). In fact, he considered the delineation of what can be said and what cannot be said, but only shown, the cardinal problem of philosophy.[1] The bulk of the *Tractatus* deals with language and logic because Wittgenstein wants to ' . . . signify what cannot be said, by presenting clearly what can be said' (T. 4.115).

[1] In replying to Russell's comments after reading the manuscript of the *Tractatus* Wittgenstein wrote, 'Now I am afraid you haven't really got hold of my main contention, to which the whole business of logical propositions is only corollary. The main point is the theory of what can be expressed by propositions—i.e. by language . . . and what cannot be expressed by propositions, but only shown; which I believe, is the cardinal problem of philosophy.' Quoted in Anscombe, op. cit., p. 161.

We have seen what 'can be said' according to the *Tractatus*: that, and that only, 'can be said' which is capable of being true or false, so that which of the two possibilities is actual has to be decided by 'comparing the proposition with reality'. A proposition has 'sense' in so far as it is a logical picture of the world. But no picture can be true *a priori*. 'It is impossible to tell from the picture alone whether it is true or false' (T. 2.224) without comparing it with reality. Logical propositions are true *a priori*, they are tautologies (T. 6.1) and their negations are contradictions. Thus, ' . . . the propositions of logic say nothing' (T. 6.11), they are senseless (T. 4.461). Nevertheless they are not nonsensical, for they *show* ' . . . the formal-logical-properties of language and the world' (T. 6.12), or the limit of language and the world.

What about the propositions of philosophy? Philosophical propositions are neither 'empirical' nor 'logical', they are, according to Wittgenstein, attempts to say things which cannot be said. 'Most of the propositions and questions to be found in philosophical works are not false but nonsensical. Consequently, we cannot give any answer to questions of this kind, but can only establish that they are nonsensical. Most of the propositions and questions arise from our failure to understand the logic of our language. (They belong to the same class as the question whether the good is more or less identical than the beautiful)' (T. 4.003). This judgment on traditional philosophy follows automatically once we understand 'the logic of our language' as shown by the *Tractatus*. According to the *Tractatus* theory of 'the logic of our language', all that can be said is *how* reality is (i.e. that certain atomic facts exist and that certain others do not); nothing can be significantly said about *what* reality is (T. 3.221), which is precisely what metaphysicians attempt to talk about.

Religion, ethics, art and the realm of the personal are, like metaphysics, concerned with what cannot be said—that which transcends the world. 'The sense of the world must lie outside the world. In the world everything is as it is, and everything happens as it does happen: *in* it no value exists. ... For all that happens and is the case is accidental. What makes it non-accidental cannot lie *within* the world. ... It must lie outside the world (T. 6.41). And so it is impossible for there to be propositions of ethics. Propositions can express nothing of what is higher' (T. 6.42). Wittgenstein considered ethics and aesthetics one and the same, they are both transcendental (T. 6.421); and so is religion and '*How* things are in the world is a matter of complete indifference for what is higher. God does not reveal himself *in* the world' (T. 6.432). 'The solution of the riddle of life in space and time lies *outside* space and time. (It is certainly not the solution of any problems of natural science that is required)' (T. 6.4312). Thus, concludes Wittgenstein, 'There are, indeed, things that are inexpressible. They *show* themselves. They are what is mystical' (T. 6.522).[1]

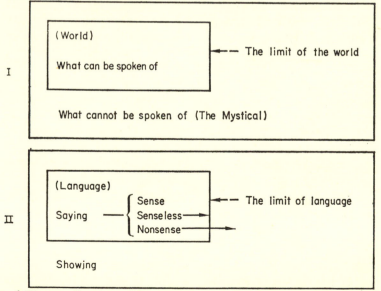

---

[1] The wording here differs slightly from the Pears and McGuinness translation.

The relation between 'what can be said' and 'what cannot be said' can be clearly represented by the diagrams shown opposite.

Diagram II is the 'mirror-image' of diagram I. It should be pointed out that 'sense', 'senseless' and 'nonsense' are terms applicable solely to 'saying'—i.e. propositions. We can say things with *sense* only *within the limits* of language. Attempts to say anything *about the limit* of language result in senseless propositions, and attempts to say anything about *what lies on the other side of the limit* end in *nonsense*. 'Sense', 'senseless' and 'nonsense' are primarily logical categories, but they are also used in the ordinary sense with evaluative connotation.[1] The failure to understand Wittgenstein's distinctions results in misinterpreting the *Tractatus* as an anti-metaphysical treatise. That the earlier commentators and readers of the *Tractatus* did not appreciate Wittgenstein's important distinction between 'senseless' (sinnlos) and 'nonsensical' (unsinnig) is evident from the first English edition of the book in which 'unsinnig' (nonsensical) is often translated as 'senseless'—the same translation given to 'sinnlos'.

Logical positivists characteristically regarded the *Tractatus* as the crystallization of their own anti-metaphysical doctrines. As Carnap reports, years later, 'When we were reading Wittgenstein's book in the Circle, I had erroneously believed that his attitude toward metaphysics was similar to ours. I had not paid sufficient attention to the statements in his book about the mystical, because his feelings and thoughts in this area were too divergent from mine. Only personal contact with him helped me to see more clearly his attitude at this point.'[2] Positivists considered metaphysics to be simply nonsense and hence to be eliminated. This tendency

[1] Frank Ramsey reports that some of Wittgenstein's terms are intentionally ambiguous, having an ordinary and a special meaning. (According to Ramsey's letter to his mother written on September 20th, 1923 while visiting Wittgenstein. Included in von Hayek, *Unfinished Sketch*.)

[2] R. Carnap, 'Autobiography', in *The Philosophy of Rudolph Carnap* (La Salle, Illinois, 1964). p. 27. Also in Fann (ed.), op. cit., p. 36.

remains in recent interpretations of the *Tractatus*. For example Pitcher contends that the statements of the *Tractatus*
implies: 'metaphysics is to be eliminated'.[1] The same
misunderstanding prompted Stenius to say, 'On the one
hand the "inexpressible", . . . has a positive ring, but on the
other hand Wittgenstein seems to share the positivistic
tendency to regard it as nonsense which does not deserve
our attention. . . . And . . . we have a definite feeling that
what is inexpressible is just nonsense and nothing else.'[2]

Wittgenstein has never said and would never have said,
'Metaphysics is nonsense' or 'the inexpressible (what cannot
be said) is just nonsense'. What he did say was: 'Most of the
propositions and questions to be found in philosophical works
are not false but nonsensical' (T. 4.003, my italics). His
point is simply this: Philosophical 'propositions' are not
false, they do not mis-state facts which could be correctly
stated, for they do not state or mis-state any facts at all—they
merely look like propositions but are in reality, not propositions in the strict sense. The attempt to *say* something (in
the sense of stating propositions) about what transcends the
world (the inexpressible) results in nonsense. In other words,
to present a pseudo-proposition in the guise of a genuine
proposition results in nonsense. This does not mean that
Wittgenstein was anti-metaphysical, although he was
certainly critical of the traditional metaphysical philosophers
who presented their sentences as 'propositions'. It is significant that Wittgenstein made a point of saying that most
traditional 'philosophical propositions' are nonsensical but
he did not say, for example, that poetry consists of nothing
but nonsensical propositions, although sentences in most
poems would clearly fall under that category if they are
treated as 'propositions'.[3] The reason behind this is that

---

[1] G. Pitcher, *The Philosophy of Wittgenstein* (New Jersey, 1964), p. 159
[2] E. Stenius, *Wittgenstein's 'Tractatus'* (Oxford, 1960), p. 225.
[3] After writing this I discovered: 'Do not forget that a poem, even
though it is composed in the language of information, is not used in the
language-game of giving information' (Z. §160).

poems, unlike metaphysical treatises, are not usually presented as consisting of 'propositions' which state some *truths* about the world. Now, if Wittgenstein had said, 'It is nonsense to regard a piece of poetry as a scientific treatise', it cannot be interpreted to mean, 'poetry is nonsense'. He would be drawing our attention to the important distinction between science and poetry.

For Wittgenstein, metaphysics, ethics, religion and art all belong to the realm of the transcendental which cannot be *said* but only *shown*. It would indeed be nonsense to contend as Stenius does, 'what is inexpressible is just nonsense and nothing else'. The inexpressible (or the mystical) is *everything* that is important in life. The whole point of the *Tractatus* is precisely to *show* the inexpressible by exhibiting clearly the expressible.

Against the standard interpretation of the *Tractatus* I contend that it is not anti-metaphysical. On the contrary, Wittgenstein was defending metaphysics in a way similar to a theologian's attempt to defend religion by saying, 'All attempts to *prove* the existence of God are nonsense, for it is not a question of proof at all—it is a matter of faith.'[1] His positive attitude toward metaphysics (and religion) is clearly shown in Carnap's report: 'Once when Wittgenstein talked about religion, the contrast between his and Schlick's position became strikingly apparent. Both agreed of course in the view that the doctrines of religion in their various forms had no theoretical content. But Wittgenstein rejected Schlick's view that religion belonged to the childhood phase of humanity and would slowly disappear in the course of cultural development. When Schlick, on another occasion, made a critical remark about a metaphysical statement by a classical philosopher (I think it was Schopenhauer),

[1] Malcolm reports: 'He was impatient with "proofs" of the existence of God, and with attempts to give religion *rational* foundation. When I once quoted to him a remark of Kierkegaard's to this effect: "How can it be that Christ does not exist, since I know that he has saved me?", Wittgenstein exclaimed: "You see! It isn't a question of *proving* anything!" ' Op. cit., p. 71.

Wittgenstein surprisingly turned against Schlick and defended the philosopher and his work.'[1]

Wittgenstein's positive attitude towards the mystical is abundantly substantiated by recent publication of Wittgenstein's 'Lecture on Ethics' and Waismann's 'Notes on Talks with Wittgenstein'.[2] He is reported to have said in 1929, 'Man has the urge to thrust against the limits of language. Think for instance about one's astonishment that anything exists. This astonishment cannot be expressed in the form of a question and there is no answer to it. Anything we can say must, *a priori*, be only nonsense. Nevertheless we thrust against the limits of language. . . . But the tendency, the thrust, *points to something*. . . . I can only say: I don't belittle this human tendency; I take my hat off to it. . . . For me the facts are unimportant. But what men mean when they say that "*The world exists*" lies close to my heart.'[3] And he concluded his lecture on ethics with the following: 'My whole tendency and I believe the tendency of all men who ever tried to write or talk Ethics or Religion was to run against the boundaries of language. This running against the walls of our cage is perfectly, absolutely hopeless. Ethics, so far as it springs from the desire to say something about the ultimate meaning of life, the absolute good, the absolute valuable, can be no science. What it says does not add to our knowledge in any sense. But it is a document of a tendency in the human mind which I personally cannot help respecting deeply and I would not for my life ridicule it.'[4] There is no doubt that his attitude toward metaphysics is the same.

---

[1] R. Carnap, op. cit., pp. 26–27.

[2] Both published in *Philosophical Review* 74, No. 1 (1965), pp. 3–16.

[3] Ibid., pp. 13–16; and in *Wittgenstein und der Wiener Kreis*, pp. 68 and 118.

[4] Ibid., pp. 11–12. I might point out a similar situation in ordinary life. When one's beloved dies there is an urge to 'communicate' with the dead by speech or writing. The attempt is absolutely hopeless but it is an expression of a tendency in the human mind which one cannot help respecting deeply; it is not something to be ridiculed.

CHAPTER IV

Philosophy

Philosophy, as we have seen, 'is not one of the natural sciences. (The word "philosophy" must mean something whose place is above or below the natural sciences, not beside them)' (T. 4.111). This follows directly from Wittgenstein's doctrine of 'what can be said'. In fact 4.111 is placed right after 4.11: 'The totality of true propositions is the whole of natural science.' Nevertheless this conclusion about philosophy was arrived at long before the composition of the *Tractatus* (in 1918). In 1913 he wrote *Notes on Logic* for Russell in which he said, 'the word "philosophy" ought to designate something over or under, but not beside, the natural sciences. Philosophy gives no pictures of reality, and can neither confirm nor confute scientific investigations. It consists of logic and metaphysics, the former its basis' (Nb. p. 93). It is apparent that Wittgenstein had very definite ideas about philosophy quite early but those ideas were not given a rationale until the 'picture theory of propositions' was clearly formulated.

Since philosophy does not give us any *truths*, what is, or ought to be, its task and function? And what is Wittgenstein doing in the *Tractatus*? His answers are stated as follows:

T. 4.112   Philosophy aims at the logical clarification of thoughts.

Philosophy is not a body of doctrine but an activity.

29

A philosophical work consists essentially of elucidations.

Philosophy does not result in 'philosophical propositions', but rather in the clarification of propositions.

Without philosophy thoughts are, as it were, cloudy and indistinct: its task is to make them clear and to give them sharp boundaries.

T. 4.113   Philosophy settles controversies about the limits of natural science.

T. 4.114   It must set limits to what can be thought; and, in doing so, to what cannot be thought.

It must set limits to what cannot be thought by working outwards through what can be thought.

T. 4.115   It will signify what cannot be said, by presenting clearly what can be said.

In the Preface Wittgenstein said, 'Thus the aim of the book is to set a limit to thought . . .' (p. 3). That is to say, to set a sharp boundary between 'what can be thought (or said)' and 'what cannot be thought'. Philosophy *before* the *Tractatus* contained propositions which are nonsensical because philosophers were misled by the surface similarity between their 'propositions' and the propositions of natural science—they fail to understand the logic of our language (T. 4.003). Philosophy *in* the *Tractatus* is an activity of clarification and elucidations. It shows the logic of our language by presenting clearly what can be said. What about philosophy *after* the *Tractatus*?[1]

T. 6.53   The correct method in philosophy would really be the following: to say nothing except what can be said, i.e. propositions of natural science—i.e.

---

[1] The distinction of the three 'philosophies' is necessary for understanding Wittgenstein's different remarks about philosophy and explains the locations of the three groupings of remarks in the text.

something that has nothing to do with philosophy —and then, whenever someone else wanted to say something metaphysical, to demonstrate to him that he had failed to give a meaning to certain signs in his propositions. Although it would not be satisfying to the other person—he would not have the feeling that we were teaching him philosophy—*this* method would be the only strictly correct one.

The only function of philosophy from now on would be a negative one—to demonstrate to someone whenever he wanted to *say* something metaphysical that his 'propositions' are nonsensical. This *ad hoc* procedure became the major preoccupation of the *Investigations* although the method he employed there is quite different. Presumably the method to be used to demonstrate to someone that his 'metaphysical propositions' are nonsensical is the method of analysis: if someone states a metaphysical proposition, you would *analyse* his proposition by asking questions such as: 'What do you mean by *this* and *that* term?' 'How do you decide whether it is true?' and 'What would it be like for it to be otherwise?' Finally he would be forced to 'spell-out' what he meant in terms of elementary propositions and then you can show him that he had failed to give a meaning to certain signs in his proposition. It should be kept in mind that this procedure is applicable only when someone wanted to *say* something metaphysical—i.e. to try to pass off a string of words *as* a factual statement which is capable of truth or falsity. If he had uttered the same string of words as a poem then to show that it does not convey any factual information is quite irrelevant.

Proper appreciation of Wittgenstein's remarks turns on remembering that 'saying', 'proposition' and other terms have very special meaning in the *Tractatus*. Thus when Wittgenstein concludes the book with, 'Whereof one cannot speak, thereof one must be silent'[1] (T. 7), it should not be surprising to anyone who has understood him up to that point. What can be *said*—i.e. the propositions of natural science, can be said clearly; What cannot be said—the mystical, can only be *shown*. To try to *say* what cannot be said but only *shown* results in nonsense; thus, we must be *silent*. This is the whole import of the famous last sentence of the *Tractatus*.

'Silence' here should not be interpreted to mean 'complete silence' in the ordinary sense of not uttering any sound. Wittgenstein considered the distinction between what can be said, and what cannot be said but only shown, to be the *main* point of the *Tractatus* and he rightfully regarded his advice, 'Whereof one cannot speak, thereof one must be silent',[2] as the *whole sense* of the book (see his Preface). 'Silence' here means 'do not *say* (in the special sense)', and therefore his advice is simply: 'Don't try to *say* what cannot be *said*' for 'What *can* be shown, *cannot* be said' (T. 4.1212).

It is clear that Ramsey's famous remark, 'But what we can't say we can't say, and we can't whistle either',[3] misses Wittgenstein's point completely. Wittgenstein's whole point is precisely this: the inexpressible—that which is really important—cannot be said (by natural sciences) but only

---

[1] Wittgenstein seems to use *sagen* (say), *reden* (talk) and *sprechen* (speak) interchangeably. For this proposition I am using C. K. Ogden's first translation instead of the more recent one.

[2] One of the founders of Logical Positivism, Otto Neurath, complained that this proposition is highly misleading. 'It sounds as if there were a "something" of which we could not speak. We should rather say, "If one really wishes to avoid the metaphysical attitude entirely, then one will 'be silent' but not 'about something'." ' Quoted from 'Sociology and Physicalism', in *Logical Positivism* (ed. A. J. Ayer), p. 284. 'Wovon man nicht sprechen kann, darüber muss man schweigen' (7). 'Wovon' means 'that which'; Wittgenstein clearly wishes to imply that there *is* something we cannot speak about. Cf. T. 6.522.

[3] F. Ramsey, *The Foundations of Mathematics* (London, 1931), p. 238.

shown (by music, art, literature, religion and what not).
There are unlimited ways to *show* the inexpressible. For
example, logic can *show* the limit of the world by arranging
symbols in a certain way.[1] Music and art can *show* something
important by arranging sounds and colours in a certain way.
Singing, acting, praying,[2] yes and even whistling are possible
ways of *showing*. The mystical *can be shown*. Wittgenstein
does not tell us much how it is shown because his central
concern in the *Tractatus* is merely to *show* that it cannot be
said. Is not this why he remarked in the preface that 'the
second thing in which the value of this book consists is that
it shows how little is achieved'?

The inescapable question must finally be raised: '*How*
does the *Tractatus show* what is shown in it? What is the
status of the "propositions" in the *Tractatus*?' Wittgenstein
answers:

T. 6.54   My propositions serve as elucidations in the
               following way: anyone who understands me
               eventually recognizes them as nonsensical, when
               he has used them—as steps—to climb up beyond
               them. (He must, so to speak, throw away the
               ladder after he has climbed up it.)
               He must transcend these propositions, and
               then he will see the world aright.

Nothing in the *Tractatus* has aroused more interest or
caused more headaches for the commentators than the
above remarks. Wittgenstein has said in the Preface that
'the *truth* of the thoughts that are here set forth seems to me
unassailable and definitive', but now he pronounces his

---

[1] 'Logical so-called propositions *shew* (the) logical properties of language and therefore of (the) Universe, but *say* nothing. This means that
by merely looking at them you can *see* these properties; whereas, in a
proposition proper, you cannot see what is true by looking at it' (Nb.
p. 67).

[2] 'To pray is to think about the meaning of life' (Nb. p. 73).

'propositions' nonsensical. Clearly there is a contradiction! Russell set the tone of criticism when he said in the Introduction, 'What causes hesitation is the fact that, after all, Mr. Wittgenstein manages to say a good deal about what cannot be said, thus suggesting to the sceptical reader that possibly there may be some loophole through a hierarchy of language, or by some other exit' (p. xxi). Since then commentators have either dismissed Wittgenstein's last remarks as self-destructive or attempted to devise ways to explain away the apparent paradox.

Criticisms of the ladder metaphor are plentiful and their line of attack can be seen by a few samples: Carnap wrote in 1935, '[Wittgenstein] seems to me to be inconsistent in what he does. He tells us that one cannot state philosophical propositions ...; and then instead of keeping silent, he writes a whole philosophical book.'[1] Winston Barnes said in 1950, 'the notion of elucidatory nonsense is one that only a very subtle mind in a very stupid moment could have conceived. It were better to be silent than to speak thus'.[2] And Pitcher contended in 1964, 'Wittgenstein considers his philosophical assertions to be illuminating nonsense. ... This evaluation cannot be accepted; Wittgenstein has said these things and therefore they can be said. What *is* nonsensical is to deny that what has been said can be said.'[3]

These remarks display a number of fundamental misunderstandings. In the first place Wittgenstein himself has never said and, I believe, never would have said that his propositions are 'important', 'elucidatory', or 'illuminating' nonsense. The phrase was wrongly attributed to Wittgenstein by Frank Ramsey when he said in 1929, 'Philosophy must be of some use and we must take it seriously; it must clear our thoughts and so our actions. Or else it is a disposition we have to check, and an inquiry to see that this is so;

[1] R. Carnap, *Philosophy and Logical Syntax* (London, 1955), pp. 37f.
[2] W. Barnes, *The Philosophical Predicament* (Boston, 1950), p. 105.
[3] Pitcher, op. cit., p. 155.

i.e. the chief proposition of philosophy is that philosophy is nonsense. And again we must then take seriously that it is nonsense, and not pretend, as Wittgenstein does, that it is important nonsense!'[1] Ramsey, although a sympathetic interpreter of Wittgenstein, is not very reliable here. This can be shown by the fact that although he assisted in the translation of the *Tractatus* the distinction between 'senseless' and 'nonsense' was not made in the English text, and by his implied attribution of the statement: 'Philosophy is non-sense' to Wittgenstein.

Just as Wittgenstein would not have said, 'Philosophy is nonsense' he could not have said, 'My propositions are illuminating (or elucidatory) nonsense.' What he did say was quite different: 'My propositions serve as elucidations in the following way: anyone who understands me eventually recognizes them as nonsensical' (T. 6.54). 'Nonsense' applies to what we *say*—i.e. propositions; it is not applicable to 'philosophy', nor can it be qualified as 'elucidatory' or 'important'. Wittgenstein's whole task in the *Tractatus* is to *show* or to *elucidate* the distinction between what can be said and what cannot be said. *How* he accomplishes this is a question we should attempt to answer.

Wittgenstein begins the *Tractatus* by saying that the *truth* of the thoughts in what follows are unassailable and definitive, but ends by saying that they are nonsense. There seems to be a clear inconsistency, but if the steps in between are given it should be apparent that nothing can emerge but T. 6.54 and 7. Here are the steps:

The aim of this book is to set a limit to thought, . . . and what lies on the other side of the limit will simply be nonsense (Preface).

[Philosophy] must set limits to what cannot be thought by working outwards through what can be thought (T. 4.114).

[1] Ramsey, op. cit., p. 263.

It will signify what cannot be said, by presenting clearly
what can be said (T. 4.115).
... what can be said—i.e. propositions of natural science
... (T. 5.53).
The totality of true propositions is the whole of natural
science (T. 4.11).
Philosophy is not one of the natural sciences (T. 4.111).
A philosophical work consists essentially of elucidations
(T. 4.112).
My propositions serve as elucidations in the following
way: Anyone who understands me eventually recognizes
them as nonsensical (T. 6.54).

Given Wittgenstein's doctrine of 'saying', the sentences of
the *Tractatus* cannot be said to 'say' anything. They, like the
propositions of other metaphysical books, cannot qualify as
'propositions' in the strict sense; and accordingly, must be
regarded as 'nonsensical'. *This* much is clear. What is not
clear is: *how* do those 'propositions' *show* the *truth* contained
in the *Tractatus*? 'Proposition', let me repeat, has a special
sense in the *Tractatus*; *propositions* have sense, they can be
true or false. Is this why Wittgenstein emphasizes the word
'truth' in the Preface where he says that the thoughts in the
book are definitely true? He, as it were, wants the reader to
treat what follows as any other traditional philosophical
treatise, as containing *truths*. (How else could he expect the
reader to treat it?) But if the reader understands him, he
will eventually recognize the 'propositions' in the *Tractatus* as
nonsensical. This is how Wittgenstein planned it. His pro-
nouncements treated *as propositions* are nonsensical. The
reader must '*transcend* these propositions, and then he will
see the world aright'. The implication is that he did not 'see
the world aright' before climbing those steps. *Something*
important is gained—i.e. 'seeing the world aright',—the
boundary between what can be said and what cannot be
said has become clear to him.

This way of *showing* is not as complicated as it seems on the outset. After all, Wittgenstein has given an analogous example a few paragraphs before concerning the meaning of life:

T. 6.52   We feel that even when *all possible* scientific questions have been answered, the problems of life remain completely untouched. Of course there are then no questions left, and this itself is the answer.

This passage has been used to support the positivistic interpretation of the *Tractatus* as asserting: 'Science is everything, everything else is nothing but nonsense.' This hasty conclusion resulted from the failure to look closely into his next sentence:

T. 6.521   The solution of the problem of life is seen in the vanishing of the problem.
              (Is not this the reason why those who have found after a long period of doubt that the sense of life became clear to them have then been unable to say what constituted that sense?)

Here, I think, Wittgenstein is describing a very common phenomenon which no doubt many have experienced. A young man who starts to reflect on life and the world is bound to ask, 'What is the purpose of life? What is the meaning of it all?' He expects a straightforward answer such as one could give to ordinary questions like 'What is the car for?' 'What is the purpose of doing exercise?' After long reflection he may detect something odd about his original question as he doesn't seem to be satisfied with *any* sort of answer, and finally he may decide that the question itself is not strictly meaningful. As Wittgenstein says, '. . . a question [exists] only where an answer exists, and an answer only where something *can be said*' (T. 6.51). No amount of scientific information can solve the problem of the meaning of life. But *after* the vanishing of the problem 'the sense of life became clear' although one is unable to say what that sense is. Thus, although the 'question' of the meaning of life is strictly speaking not a question, the *process* of raising the question, trying to answer it and finally realizing the non-sensicality of the question *shows* the meaning of life to the one who has gone through this process. He is better off for it, the sense of life becomes clear to him.

Similarly by raising questions such as, 'What is the essence of language and the world?' 'What are the limits of language and the world?' giving answers to those questions (as the *Tractatus* attempts to do), and finally recognizing that both the questions and answers are strictly speaking nonsensical; the reader is better off for it,—'he will see the world aright'. That is why the ladder can only be thrown away *after* he has climbed up on it.

PART 2

The Later Wittgenstein

The destroyer of weeds, thistles and thorns is a benefactor whether he soweth or not.

Robert G. Ingersoll

What we are destroying is nothing but houses of cards and we are clearing up the ground of language on which they stand.

Ludwig Wittgenstein

CHAPTER V

Transition

After the publication of the *Tractatus* Wittgenstein abandoned philosophy to become an elementary-school teacher
in an Austrian village. This course of action was quite
consistent with his contention in the *Tractatus* that all
essential philosophical problems were solved. Ramsey reported, '[Wittgenstein] says that he himself will do nothing
more not because he is bored but because his mind is no
longer flexible. He says no one can do more than 5 or 10
years good work at philosophy (his work took 7).'[1] It was
not until 1929 that he felt he could again do creative work
and returned to Cambridge.

It is clear from the paper 'Some Remarks on Logical
Form',[2] which he wrote for the Aristotelian Society, that he
still subscribed to the basic doctrines of the *Tractatus*.
Nevertheless this paper contains an important criticism of
the *Tractatus* which indicates the direction of his later
development. As in the *Tractatus* Wittgenstein believes that
analysis of ordinary propositions must lead to elementary
propositions. But the form of elementary propositions was
given *a priori* in the *Tractatus*; and indeed, the whole procedure of investigation was *a priori*. Now he says, 'We can

---

[1] From his letter to his mother dated September 20th, 1923. Included
in von Hayek's *Unfinished Sketch*.

[2] This was written immediately following his return to England in
1929 but was soon repudiated as new ideas which lead to the *Investigations*
were forming in his mind. See his letter to *Mind* XLII (1933) and G. E.
Moore, 'Wittgenstein's Lectures in 1930–33', p. 253.

only arrive at a correct analysis by what might be called the logical investigation of the phenomena themselves, i.e., in a certain sense *a posteriori*, and not by conjecturing about *a priori* possibilities. One is often tempted to ask from an *a priori* standpoint: What, after all, *can* be the only forms of [elementary] propositions. . . . An [elementary] form cannot be foreseen. And it would be surprising if the actual phenomena had nothing more to teach us about their structure.'[1]

The purely *a priori* method of the *Tractatus* is under attack and he now recommends (in a certain sense) the *a posteriori* method of investigating the actual phenomena of language. This shift of *methods* is what constituted the break between the early and the later Wittgenstein. An interesting fact seldom mentioned by the commentators is that some *seeds* of Wittgenstein's later philosophy were already contained in his pre-*Tractatus Notebooks*. As pointed out before he had doubts about some of his basic doctrines of the *Tractatus*. He was not even sure of his major thesis that the totality of propositions is language—'Is it a tautology to say: *Language consists of propositions*? It seems it *is*' (Nb. p. 52).[2] Nor was he certain about the picture theory; 'On the one hand my theory of logical portrayal seems to be the only possible one, on the other hand there seems to be an insoluble contradiction in it!' (Nb. p. 17). During the composition of the *Tractatus* he believed that there *must* be 'objects' but to produce examples of them was not a logician's business. However, he wrote in the *Notebooks*, 'Our difficulty was that we kept speaking of simple objects but were unable to mention a single one' (Nb. p. 68). On the other hand we find entries such as: 'I only want to justify the vagueness of ordinary propositions, for it *can* be justified' (Nb. p. 70); and, 'The

---

[1] *Aristotelian Society Proceedings*, Supp. Vol. 9 (1929), 163–4.

[2] In the *Notebooks* 'Satz' is translated as 'proposition' in some places and as 'sentence' in others but I shall translate it as 'proposition' consistently in my quotations.

way in which language signifies is mirrored in its use' (Nb. p. 82)—a most typical statement in the *Investigations*. Some of these insights are contained in the *Tractatus* without elaboration. For example, we find a parenthetical remark in T. 6.211: '(In philosophy the question, "What do we actually use this word or this sentence for?" repeatedly leads to valuable insights.)' If these remarks were taken seriously they could have led to a philosophy quite different from the *Tractatus*, for they clearly imply that we should investigate the 'actual use' of language (which is precisely the main emphasis of the *Investigations*.)

As it happened Wittgenstein followed the *a priori* method and settled with the results of the *Tractatus*. Black suggests that Wittgenstein's thoughts were in constant flux and that his position was intentionally 'frozen' for the sake of publication.[1] This explanation is wrong. From what is known about Wittgenstein's life and character, there is no doubt that he actually believed that he had solved all important philosophical problems and quit philosophy accordingly. The doubts expressed in the *Notebooks* were either suppressed or resolved at the time of the publication of the *Tractatus*. They apparently surfaced again in 1929 to haunt his tormented mind.

The years Wittgenstein spent in teaching elementary-school children may be considered the most decisive factor in the shaping of his later philosophy. The reality of teaching children how to read, write, calculate, etc., and the experience in compiling a dictionary for elementary schools[2] must have contributed to Wittgenstein's later pragmatic view of language. How else does one find out whether a child knows the meaning of a word or not except by observing how the child *uses* the word? And, doesn't the explanation of the meaning of a word to children consist precisely in teaching them the *use* of the word?

---

[1] Max Black, *A Companion to the Tractatus*, p. 23.
[2] *Wörterbuch für Volksschulen* (Vienna, 1926).

The effects of his teaching experience on his later philosophy is quite evident in both his lectures and writings. He remarked once that, in order to get clear about the meaning of a word, it is very useful to ask oneself: 'How is this word learned?' 'How would one set about teaching a child to use this word?'[1] In a lecture on aesthetics he said: 'One thing we always do when discussing a word is to ask how we were taught it. . . . Cf. How did we learn "I dreamt so and so"? The interesting point is that we didn't learn it by being shown a dream. If you ask yourself how a child learns "beautiful", "fine", etc., you find he learns them roughly as interjections. . . .'[2] In another context, writing on a similar topic, Wittgenstein asks: 'Am I doing child psychology?—I am making a connection between the concept of teaching and the concept of meaning' (Z. §412). Only an elementary-school teacher could have thought of making this connection. The consequence of this connection constitutes a most important aspect of his 'new method'. Consider his treatment of the following traditional problem:

> One man is a convinced realist, another a convinced idealist and teaches his children accordingly. In such an important matter as the existence or non-existence of the external world they don't want to teach their children anything wrong.
> What will the children be taught? To include in what they say: 'There are physical objects?' or the opposite?
> . . .
> But the idealist will teach his children the word 'chair' after all, for of course he wants to teach them to do this and that, e.g. to fetch a chair. Then where will be the difference between what the idealist-educated children say and the realist ones? (Z. §413f.).

[1] See: Gasking and Jackson, 'Wittgenstein as a Teacher', in Fann (ed.), *Wittgenstein: The Man and his Philosophy* (New York, 1967).
[2] *Lectures and Conversations*, pp. 1–2.

We might also ask: What will be the difference between what the determinist children say and the libertarian ones? etc. No doubt Wittgenstein would approve of the pragmatic dictum: A difference that makes no difference is not a real difference. It would not be an exaggeration to say that the early Wittgenstein's ivory tower view of language was brought down to earth by his elementary-school pupils.

The immediate circumstances of his shift from the *Tractatus* to the *Investigations*, however, was largely due to criticism by Frank Ramsey and Piero Sraffa, an Italian economist teaching at Cambridge. In the preface to the *Investigations*, Wittgenstein acknowledges the effectiveness of the criticism which forced him 'to recognize grave mistakes' in the *Tractatus*. He refers to discussions of these in 'innumerable conversations with Ramsey, during the last two years of his life . . .'[1] and to the forcible criticism that Sraffa 'for many years unceasingly practised' on his thoughts; and acknowledged: 'I am indebted to *this* stimulus for the most consequential ideas of this book.' He said, according to von Wright, that his discussions with Sraffa made him feel like a tree from which all branches had been cut.[2] In both cases the criticism is merely acknowledged without any indication of its character. Since no record of these discussions is available, we can only guess at their general nature.

The nature of Ramsey's criticism can be gathered from some of his essays posthumously collected in a single volume.[3] In 'Facts and Propositions' Ramsey says, 'I must emphasize my indebtedness to Mr. Wittgenstein, from whom my view of logic is derived. Everything that I have

[1] Ramsey died in 1930 at the age of 27. Moore mentions in 'Wittgenstein's Lectures 1930–33', n. 1, that Wittgenstein was mistaken about the number of years. It should be 'one' instead.

[2] In Malcolm op. cit., p. 16.

[3] *The Foundations of Mathematics* (London, Routledge & Kegan Paul, 1931).

said is due to him, except the parts which have a pragmatist tendency, which seem to me to be needed in order to fill up a gap in his system. . . . My pragmatism is . . . very vague and undeveloped. The essence of pragmatism I take to be this, that the meaning of a sentence is to be defined by reference to the actions to which asserting it would lead, or more vaguely still, by its possible causes and effects. Of this I feel certain, but of nothing more definite' (1927).[1]

In his paper 'Philosophy' (1929), Ramsey writes: 'The chief danger to our philosophy, apart from laziness and wooliness, is *scholasticism*, the essence of which is treating what is vague as if it were precise and trying to fit it into an exact logical category. A typical piece of scholasticism is Wittgenstein's view that all our everyday propositions are completely in order and that it is impossible to think illogically.'[2] The cause of scholasticism lies in the method of philosophy. We 'construct a logic, and do all our philosophical analysis entirely *unself-consciously*, thinking all the time of the facts and not about our thinking about them, deciding what we mean without any reference to the nature of meanings.'[3] This logical method of analysis is unsatisfactory because 'in the process of clarifying our thought we come to terms and sentences which we cannot elucidate in the obvious manner by defining their meaning. . . . [But] we can explain the way in which they are used, and in this explanation we are forced to look not only at the objects which we are talking about, but at our own mental states.'[4] Hence Ramsey recommends that we should regain self-consciousness in philosophy—we must pay attention to 'the epistemic or subjective side' of the matter. In contrast

---

[1] Ibid., p. 155. Ramsey derived his pragmatism from its founder—C. S. Peirce (see p. 194, n. 2). The indirect (through Ramsey) influence of Peirce's pragmatism on Wittgenstein is apparent in all of his later writings and specifically in the *Investigations* §81: 'Ramsey once emphasized in conversation with me that logic was a "normative science" [Peirce's phrase] . . .'   [2] Ibid., p. 269.
[3] Ibid., p. 267.   [4] Ibid.

RAMSEY

with the *Tractatus*, the examination of epistemological and psychological concepts is of central importance in the *Investigations*.

From the remarks quoted above, it is not difficult to see what Ramsey's contribution to the later development of Wittgenstein consisted in. The decidedly pragmatic tendency in Wittgenstein's later work contrasts most sharply with his earlier theoretic approach. This pragmatic attitude has another source—viz. William James. James's *Principles of Psychology* was one of the very few books he used as a kind of textbook in his lectures.[1] Drury reports, 'Wittgenstein had a great admiration for James, and the *Varieties of Religious Experience* was one of the few books he insisted I must read.'[2] The reason for Wittgenstein's admiration is not difficult to find. At the beginning of his second lecture on *The Varieties of Religious Experience*, James writes that 'Most books on the philosophy of religion try to begin with a precise definition of what its essence consists of'; and a little later says: 'The theorizing mind always tends to the oversimplification of its materials. This is the root of all that absolutism and one-sided dogmatism by which both philosophy and religion have been infested. Let us not fall immediately into a one-sided view of our subject but let us rather admit freely at the outset that we may very likely find no one essence, but many characters which may alternately be equally important to religion.' And in his first lecture he says, 'To understand a thing rightly we need to see it both out of its environment and in it', and 'it always leads to a better understanding of a thing's significance to consider its exaggerations and per-

[1] It is well known that he did not use 'textbooks' in any ordinary sense. Nevertheless, W. Mays reports, 'When he was lecturing on belief he read extracts from James' *Principles of Psychology*, and discussed them critically.' In K. T. Fann (ed.), op. cit. p. 83. This is confirmed by numerous references to James in students' notes of Wittgenstein's lectures. Cf. references to James in P.I. §342, §413, §610, p. 219.

[2] 'Ludwig Wittgenstein: A Symposium', in Fann (ed.), op. cit., p. 68.

versions, its equivalents and substitutes and nearest relatives elsewhere'.[1]

These remarks and suggestions could be inserted into the *Investigations* without oddness. Wittgenstein's attack on essentialism, his notion of family-resemblance, his use of the extreme examples, and his emphasis on 'circumstances', are certainly close relatives to James's ideas. The targets of James's attack: the theorizing mind, over-simplification, the one-sided view, dogmatism, and the search for 'one essence' are precisely the characteristics of the early Wittgenstein.

The nature of Sraffa's criticism is not clear as he has not written anything on Wittgenstein or on philosophy.[2] The only thing which suggests something of the character of Sraffa's criticism is an anecdote told to Malcolm by Wittgenstein. According to Malcolm, 'One day . . . when Wittgenstein was insisting that a proposition and that which it describes must have the same "logical form," and the same "logical multiplicity", Sraffa made a gesture familiar to Neopolitans as meaning something like disgust or contempt, of brushing the underneath of his chin with an outward sweep of the fingertips of one hand. Sraffa's example produced in Wittgenstein the feeling that there was an absurdity in the insistence that a proposition and what it describes must have the same "form". This broke the hold on him of the conception that a proposition must literally be a "picture" of the reality it describes.'[3] Although this particular criticism in itself does not constitute a decisive 'counter-example' (for according to the *Tractatus*, the gesture does not constitute a 'proposition'), it was probably a series of this *kind* of concrete counter-examples which broke the hold on

[1] Quoted by J. Wisdom in 'A Feature of Wittgenstein's Technique', in Fann (ed.), op. cit., p. 353.

[2] In a letter to the author dated March 2nd, 1966, he says, 'I am an incredibly slow writer on my own subject of economics and I have never written anything on philosophy or Wittgenstein. If I ever tried this I doubt that I should ever complete it. . . .'

[3] Malcolm, op. cit., p. 69.

Wittgenstein of the conception that language always functions in *one* way. What is important about the gesture
described above is its *use* in concrete circumstances. In contrast with the *Tractatus* where he was mainly concerned with
the cognitive use of language, the later Wittgenstein stressed
the expressive aspects such as gestures, etc., whose meanings
are determined by social contexts and concrete situations.[1]
As 'use' becomes more important, so do the users and hence
the society.

Sraffa's contribution to the development of the later
Wittgenstein must be more than his 'forcible' criticism,
otherwise Wittgenstein would not have said that he was
indebted to Sraffa's stimulus for the most consequential
ideas of the *Investigations*. A glimpse of Sraffa's positive
contribution may be detected in his only published work,
Production of Commodities by Means of Commodities (Prelude to
a Critique of Economic Theory).[2] In this short (100 pages)
work on economics, Sraffa utilizes what Mays called 'the
method of speculative anthropology'[3] which Wittgenstein
uses extensively in his lectures and writings. Sraffa starts
his investigation of the process of production with an
imaginary society: 'Let us consider an extremely simple
society which produces just enough to maintain itself. . . .
Suppose at first that only two commodities are produced
. . .',[4] and then builds up the more complicated forms by
gradually adding new features. This method, central to
Sraffa's whole investigation, is also quite central to Wittgenstein's later work. The important method of imagining and

---

[1] Cf. W. Mays, 'Recollections of Wittgenstein', in Fann (ed.), op.
cit., p. 83.

[2] Cambridge University Press, 1960. Although it was not published
until 1960, 'the central propositions had taken shape in the late 1920's'
(Preface), and a draft of Part I was written before 1928; that is to say,
before he met Wittgenstein.

[3] W. Mays, 'Recollections of Wittgenstein' in Fann (ed.), op. cit.,
p. 83.

[4] Sraffa, op. cit., p. 3.

constructing simple and complicated 'language-games' seems to be an adaptation of Sraffa's method. In the *Blue Book* Wittgenstein writes, 'I shall in the future again and again draw your attention to what I shall call language-games. These are ways of using signs simpler than those in which we use the signs of our highly complicated everyday language. . . . The study of language-games is the study of primitive forms of language or primitive languages. . . . When we look at such simple forms of language the mental mist which seems to enshroud our ordinary use of language disappears. . . . We see that we can build up the complicated forms from the primitive ones by gradually adding new forms' (B.B. p. 17).

In light of the above, von Wright's statement that Wittgenstein's later philosophy is 'entirely outside any philosophical tradition'[1] should not be taken without qualification. Nor can we accept his statement that although the friendship between Moore and Wittgenstein lasted until the latter's death 'there is [not] any trace of an influence of Moore's philosophy on Wittgenstein'.[2] In the preface to his *Principia Ethica* (which Wittgenstein read) Moore writes:

> It appears to me that in Ethics, as in all other philosophical studies, the difficulties and disagreements, of which its history is full, are mainly due to a very simple cause: namely to the attempt to answer questions, without first discovering precisely *what* question it is which you desire to answer. I do not know how far this source of error would be done away, if philosophers would *try* to discover what question they were asking, before they set about to answer it; for the work of analysis and distinction is often very difficult: we may often fail to make the necessary discovery, even though we make a definite attempt to do so. But . . . if only this attempt were made, many of the most glaring difficulties and disagreements in philo-

---

[1] In Fann (ed.), op. cit., p. 23.   [2] Ibid.

sophy would disappear. At all events, philosophers ... are constantly endeavouring to prove that 'Yes' or 'No' will answer questions, to which *neither* answer is correct. ... [1]

Moore's idea of 'questioning the question' through careful *analysis* and *distinction* of ordinary usage and his persistent defence of common sense are also conspicuously present in Wittgenstein's later work. It is true that Wittgenstein later criticized Moore's 'defence of common sense' as 'child-like' but he admitted that it was an important idea for it destroyed premature solutions of philosophical problems.[2] It is also true that he later criticized *analysis*—the common method of Russell, the early Wittgenstein and the Logical Positivists; but he appreciated the method of *distinction*—a method Moore alone, among all British philosophers at that time, practised. Malcolm reports that Wittgenstein, 'observed that if one were trying to find exactly the right words to express a fine distinction of thought, Moore was absolutely the best person to consult'.[3] In the *Tractatus* Wittgenstein's whole method was 'logical analysis' which he inherited from Russell, but the central method of the *Investigations* may appropriately be called the method of *distinction*. Instead of looking for *similarities* by analysis he now concentrates on uncovering *differences* by *distinction*. In fact he thought of using as a motto for the *Investigations* a quotation from King Lear: 'I'll teach you differences.'[4]

There is another important source of influence which is seldom mentioned by the commentators. Heinrich Hertz's work was always a source of inspiration for Wittgenstein—a debt he acknowledged in both his early and later writings.[5] In the introduction to his *The Principles of Mechanics*, Hertz writes:

[1] Cambridge University Press, 1903.
[2] See Malcolm, op. cit., pp. 66–7. [3] Ibid., p. 67.
[4] 'Ludwig Wittgenstein: A Symposium', in Fann (ed.), op. cit., p. 69.
[5] See T. 4.04, 6.361, and B.B. p. 36.

Weighty evidence seems to be furnished by the statements which one hears with wearisome frequency, that the nature of force is still a mystery, that one of the chief problems of physics is the investigation of the nature of force, and so on. In the same way electricians are continually attacked as to the nature of electricity. Now, why is it that people never in this way ask what is the nature of gold, or what is the nature of velocity? I fancy the difference must lie in this. With the terms 'velocity' and 'gold' we connect a large number of relations to other terms; and between all these relations we find no contradictions which offend us. We are therefore satisfied and ask no further questions. But we have accumulated around the terms 'force' and 'electricity' more relations than can be completely reconciled amongst themselves. We have an obscure feeling of this and want to have things cleared up. Our confused wish finds expression in the confused question as to the nature of force and electricity. But the answer which we want is not really an answer to this question. It is not by finding out more and fresh relations and connections existing between those already known, and thus perhaps by reducing their number. When these painful contradictions are removed, the question as to the nature of force will not have been answered; but our minds, no longer vexed, will cease to ask illegitimate questions. . . . We are convinced, . . . that the existing defects are only defects in form; and that all indistinctness and uncertainty can be avoided by suitable arrangement of definitions and notations, and by due care in the mode of expression. . . .[1]

This long quotation is given here because Hertz's conception of the nature of the problems in philosophy of science and his suggested method of solution (or rather *dis*solution)

---

[1] H. Hertz, *The Principles of Mechanics*; translated from the original edition of 1894 by De. E. Jones and J. T. Walley (New York, Dover Publications, 1956), pp. 7–9.

seem to be exactly like those of Wittgenstein with regard to philosophy in general. Wittgenstein also considered philosophical problems as "vexations" caused by contradictory relations we have accumulated around certain key terms such as 'knowledge', 'mind', 'cause', and so on. What is required for solution is not more and fresh facts but 'suitable arrangement' of what is already known and 'due care in the mode of expression'.

Other possible influences on Wittgenstein may be mentioned here. In addition to Hertz, his favourite scientific authors were Maxwell, Boltzmann, and especially the psychologist Otto Weininger. He esteemed George Lichtenberg's aphorisms highly[1] and was familiar with Fritz Mauthner's work on the critique of language.[2] It is well known that Wittgenstein was not well read in the classics of philosophy. But he did read Spinoza, Hume and Kant. And, significantly, he read and enjoyed Plato, whose philosophic method is strikingly similar to Wittgenstein's own. Of more importance to him, however, were writers in the borderland between philosphy and religion: St. Augustine, Pascal, Kierkegaard, Dostoievsky, and Tolstoy. He begins his *Investigations* with a quotation from St. Augustine's *Confessions* (which he read in Latin) not because he could not find the conception expressed in it stated as well by other philosophers, but because 'the conception *must* be important if so great a mind held it'.[3] And once he told a friend that he considered Kierkegaard to be by far the greatest philosopher of the nineteenth century.[4] Of equal importance to Wittgenstein were probably Karl Kraus and

---

[1] See Georg H. von Wright, 'Georg Christoph Lichtenberg als Philosoph'. *Theoria* 8 (1942). Cf. G. E. Moore, 'Wittgenstein's Lectures in 1930–33', in his *Philosophical Papers* (London, 1959), p. 309.

[2] See Gershon Weiler, 'On Fritz Mauthner's Critique of Language.' *Mind* 67 (1958), 80–7. Cf. T. 4.0031.

[3] Malcolm, op. cit., p. 71.

[4] See Fann (ed.), op. cit., p. 70.

Adolf Loos, two of his distinguished Viennese contemporaries. The basic affinity of his ideas with those of two apparently very diverse authors is clearly shown by Kraus's statement: 'All that Adolf Loos and I—he materially and I verbally—have ever meant to say is that there is a difference between an urn and a chamber-pot.'[1]

Another factor may contribute to our understanding of the transition. The early Wittgenstein philosophized in solitude, and the results were pronounced in a monologue. One gets the impression from reading the *Tractatus* that the propositions in it are to be accepted and not questioned. His tone rings like the tone of a man possessed by the truth. Even in conversation, Carnap reports, Wittgenstein's every pronouncement 'stood before us like a newly created piece of art or a divine revelation'.[2] The later philosophy, on the other hand, arose from discussions and lectures in which the Socratic method was employed. Wittgenstein used to emphasize that his method could not be learned by hearing lectures: discussion was essential.[3] Consequently the *Investigations* takes the form of a dialogue.

I have traced and documented *some* of the forces which contributed to the development of the later Wittgenstein with the purpose of bringing out sharply the contrasts between the *Tractatus* and the *Investigations*. It is well to remember Wittgenstein's advice that the *Investigations* 'could be seen in the right light only by contrast with and against the background of my old way of thinking'. To understand and to appreciate this contrast is already to have grasped the spirit of the *Investigations*.

---

[1] See: Paul Engelmann, *Letters from Ludwig Wittgenstein with a Memoir* (Oxford, 1967); and W. Kraft, 'Ludwig Wittgenstein und Karl Kraus', *Die Neue Rundschau* 72 (1961). For more details on this paragraph see Malcolm, op. cit.

[2] R. Carnap, op. cit., p. 26.

[3] G. E. Moore, op. cit., p. 322.

CHAPTER VI

Repudiation of Analysis

The period between his return to Cambridge and 1932 was for Wittgenstein one of continuous development and struggle. His thoughts can be seen in the *Philosophische Bemerkungen* and in Moore's notes of 'Wittgenstein's Lectures in 1930–33'. By 1933 he had rejected the *Tractatus* conception of language—the picture theory as well as the theory of truth-functions. The *Blue Book* of 1933–34 testifies to his complete transition from the early work to a radically new philosophy which culminated in the *Investigations*.

The later Wittgenstein came to regard the method and doctrines of the *Tractatus* as a paradigm of traditional philosophy. Throughout his later writings the presuppositions and views of the *Tractatus* served as the main targets of his attack. It is therefore necessary to understand the specific criticisms of the *Tractatus* contained in his later works.

The *Tractatus* was concerned with explaining '*How* language is possible'. Ordinary propositions are vague but they serve our purposes because, according to the early Wittgenstein, they are *really* quite clear and distinct. This was shown by *analysis*. Every proposition can be analysed into a set of elementary propositions which are composed of names signifying simple objects. It was believed that there must be a 'final analysis' in which all propositions are resolved into elementary propositions. This view came under attack shortly after his return to philosophy. In conversation with Schlick and Waismann in 1931, Wittgenstein said:

Much more dangerous (than dogmatism) is another error which also pervades my whole book—the notion that there are questions the answers to which will be discovered at some later date. (I recognized that we cannot make *a priori* assumptions about the forms of elementary propositions) but I thought nonetheless that it would at some later time be possible to give a list of the elementary propositions. Only in recent years have I freed myself from this error. At the time, I wrote in the manuscript of my book, though it wasn't printed in the *Tractatus*, 'The solutions of philosophical questions must never come as a surprise. In philosophy nothing can be discovered.' However, I myself did not yet understand this sufficiently clearly and made the very mistake that it attacks'.[1]

According to Moore, Wittgenstein said in one of his first lectures that it was with regard to elementary propositions and their connections with truth-functions that he had to change his opinions most.[2] He began by pointing out that he had produced no examples of elementary propositions and that there was something wrong indicated by this fact, though it was difficult to say what. His view at that time was that it was senseless to talk of a 'final' analysis. But specific criticisms were not given until the composition of the *Investigations*.

[1] Taken from notes made by Waismann, published in B. F. Mc-Guiness' 'The Mysticism of the *Tractatus*', *Philosophical Review* 75 (1966), p. 313. [German version in *Wittgenstein und der Wiener Kreis*, p. 182]. It is interesting and puzzling to note that Wittgenstein was in a habit of writing down philosophical remarks which he himself did not yet understand fully. This may account for the appearance of some remarks, full of insight but unelaborated, in his early writings which seem more appropriately to belong to his later work (such as: 'The way in which language signifies is mirrored in its use', 'if a sign is useless, it is meaningless' (T. 3.328), and 'In philosophy the question "what do we actually use this sentence for?" repeatedly leads to valuable insights').

[2] Moore, 'Wittgenstein's Lectures 1930–33', op. cit., p. 296.

In the *Investigations*, Wittgenstein not only criticizes the basic assumptions of the *Tractatus*, but also discusses the sort of considerations that led to those assumptions. One of the basic assumptions in the *Tractatus* is that every proposition has a perfectly determinate or definite sense which can be set out clearly (T. 3.251). Why does it seem necessary that every proposition must have a definite sense?

> The sense of a proposition—one would like to say—may, of course, leave this or that open, but the proposition must nevertheless have *a* definite sense. An indefinite sense—that would really not be a sense *at all*.—This is like: An indefinite boundary is not really a boundary at all. Here one thinks perhaps: if I say 'I have locked the man up fast in the room—there is only one door left open'—then I simply haven't locked him in at all; his being locked in is a sham. One would be inclined to say here: 'You haven't done anything at all.' An enclosure with a hole in it is as good as *none*.—But is that true? (P.I. §99).[1]

That every proposition must have a definite sense was an assumption the early Wittgenstein inherited from Frege. Frege contends that a vague concept is not a concept at all just as an area with blurred boundaries cannot be called an area at all. This, observed Wittgenstein, presumably means that we cannot do anything with it. But—'Is an indistinct photograph a picture of a person at all? Is it even always an advantage to replace an indistinct picture by a sharp one? Isn't the indistinct one often exactly what we need?' (P.I. §71).

Wittgenstein now realizes that his earlier view about propositions was '*not a result of investigation*: it was a requirement' (P.I. §107). His conception of language had required that every proposition should have a definite sense. This

---

[1] Anscombe translates 'Satz' as 'sentence', but 'proposition' is preferable here.

was a 'preconceived idea' about propositions which prevented clear vision 'like a pair of glasses on our nose through which we see whatever we look at. It never occurs to us to take them off' (P.I. §103). We must take off the glasses and remove the preconceived idea by 'turning our whole examination round. (One might say: the axis of reference of our examination must be rotated, but about the fixed point of our real need)' (P.I. §108).[1]

What do we find when we shed the preconceived idea? We find, says Wittgenstein, that the facts of language do not conform to our *a priori* requirement. 'The more narrowly we examine actual language, the sharper becomes the conflict between it and our requirement' (P.I. §107). We find that in actual language many propositions are vague, inexact, and indefinite but serve our purposes perfectly well. 'If I tell someone "Stand roughly here"—may not this explanation work perfectly? And cannot every other one fail too?' (P.I. §88). Someone might criticize this explanation as 'inexact' but what does 'inexact' mean here? It certainly does not mean 'unusable'. And what would an 'exact' explanation look like? It is conceivable that there are several ways in which such an order might be refined: e.g. draw a chalk line around the area indicated. But the line has breadth so a colour edge would be even more exact. But what is the purpose, in the circumstances, of striving for such increased exactness? 'Isn't the engine idling?' asks Wittgenstein.

Besides, 'inexact' and 'exact' are relative terms. 'Inexact' is used as a reproach and 'exact' is used in praise. Statements of exactness or inexactness are made in relation to a goal or a standard within a given field (or language-game). What is inexact attains its goal less perfectly than what is more exact. No single ideal (or absolute standard) of exactness has been laid down. What is considered exact in following a recipe might be considered terribly inexact in filling a pre-

[1] This 'turning round' of the axis of reference about the fixed point of our *real need* constituted his turn from 'theoretic' to 'pragmatic' approach.

scription. There is no point in criticizing the cook for failing to match the druggist's standards of exactness.

Intimately connected with the assumption that every proposition must have a definite sense was the assumption that the process of *analysis* makes the sense of the proposition explicit and clear. The method of analysis was absolutely essential to the whole doctrine of the *Tractatus*. It was quite correct to call the early Wittgenstein an 'analytic' philoso- pher and his philosophy was very appropriately classified as 'analytic'—along with Russell's, Moore's and the Positivists'. However, the notion of analysis is now under severe criticism. Suppose I say: 'My broom is in the corner', —is this really a statement about the broomstick and the brush? It is true, that the broom consists of two parts, but does someone who says: (a) 'The broom is in the corner', really mean: (b) 'The broomstick is in the corner, the brush is in the corner, and the broomstick is attached to the brush?' Wittgenstein characteristically answers:

> If we were to ask anyone if he meant this he would prob- ably say that he had not thought specially of the broom- stick or specially of the brush at all. And that would be the *right* answer, for he meant to speak neither of the stick nor of the brush in particular. Suppose that, instead of saying 'Bring me the broom', you said, 'Bring me the broomstick and the brush which is fitted on to it!'—Isn't the answer: 'Do you want the broom? Why do you put it so oddly?' (P.I. §60).

Analytical philosophers want to call (b) a 'further analysed' form of (a) in the sense that (b) *expresses* more clearly the meaning of (a). This, as Wittgenstein points out, readily reduces us into thinking that the former is the more funda- mental form and that if we have only the unanalysed form we miss that analysis. But, looking at the matter from a different point of view, can we not say that an aspect of the matter is lost in the 'analysed' form as well? (P.I. §63).

It is true, Wittgenstein points out, that sometimes mis-understandings 'can be removed by substituting one form of expression for another; this may be called an "analysis" of our forms of expression' (P.I. §90). Analysis is thus useful in some cases. However, we may be tempted to think that the 'further analysed' forms of an expression can be further and further analysed until we come to a 'final analysis' in which the expression is completely clarified and all vagueness eliminated. 'It can be put like this: we eliminate misunderstandings by making our expressions more exact; but now it may look as if we were moving towards a particular state, a state of complete exactness; and as if this were the real goal of our investigation' (P.I. §91).[1] Here Wittgenstein is clearly referring to his earlier belief that our ordinary expressions were, essentially, unanalysed; and that the sense of every expression could be completely spelled out in terms of 'elementary propositions'.

The belief in a 'final analysis' is closely connected with the assumption in the *Tractatus*, that the distinction between the simple and the complex is an absolute one—that a thing is, apart from context and without qualification, either simple or complex. The purpose of analysis is to resolve the complex proposition which describes a complex fact, into the simplest (or elementary) propositions which describe the simplest (or atomic) facts. It was assumed that the simplest proposition consists of names denoting absolutely simple things— Wittgenstein's 'objects' and Russell's 'individuals' (P.I. §46)[2]—which are the simple constituent parts of reality.

[1] An example from *Zettel* will illustrate this point: 'The regulation of traffic in the streets permits and forbids certain actions on the part of the drivers and pedestrians; but it does not attempt to guide the totality of their movements by prescription. And it would be senseless to talk of an "ideal" ordering of traffic which should do that; in the first place we should have no idea what to imagine as this ideal. If someone wants to make traffic regulations stricter on some point or other, that does not mean that he wants to approximate to such an ideal' (Z. §440).

[2] And we might add: Descartes' 'substance', Leibnitz's 'monads,'

Now Wittgenstein asks: 'What are the simple constituent parts of a chair?—The bits of wood of which it is made? Or the molecules, or the atoms?' and answers: ' "Simple" means: not composite. And here the point is: in what sense "composite"? It makes no sense at all to speak absolutely of the "simple parts of a chair" ' (P.I. §47).

'Simple' and 'complex' like 'exact' and 'inexact' are relative terms. It makes sense to speak of something as simple or complex only in a context. In a certain context a thing may be called simple, but in another context, the same thing may be considered complex. In one sense we may say that a chessboard is composed of thirty-two white and thirty-two black squares and in that sense we may consider the chessboard 'complex' and the squares 'simple'. But in a different context we might want to describe the chessboard as being composed of the colours black and white and the scheme of squares. And is the colour of a square simple, or does it consist of pure white and pure yellow? Furthermore, is pure white simple, or does it consist of the colours of the rainbow?

The point is this: simplicity and complexity are not absolute qualities inhering in the thing itself. We use the words 'simple' and 'complex' in an enormous number of different ways relative to different contexts. To ask 'Is this object complex?' without context, or 'outside a particular language-game', is reminiscent, says Wittgenstein, of a boy who had to say whether the verbs in certain sentences were in the active or passive voice, and who racked his brains over the question whether the verb 'to sleep' is active or passive (P.I. §47). Wittgenstein regards it as a typical mistake of philosophers to speak of things in absolute terms apart from all contexts. 'To the *philosophical* question: "Is the visual image of this tree composite, and what are its com-

Locke's 'ideas', Hume's 'impressions', and the Logical Positivists' 'sense-datum'.

ponent parts?'' The correct answer is: "That depends on what you understand by 'composite'.'' (And that is of course not an answer but a rejection of the question)' (P.I. §47).

Wittgenstein has clearly rejected the meaningfulness of talking about the absolutely simple 'objects', the existence of 'elementary propositions', and the notion of a 'final analysis'. 'Analysis' is no longer the main philosophical method for him. Elsewhere he ridicules the analyst as someone who 'tried to find the real artichoke by stripping it of its leaves' (B.B. p. 125; also, P.I. §164).[1] It is puzzling to see that Wittgenstein, in spite of his clear and forceful rejection of analysis, is generally classified as an "analytic" philosopher. Whatever he may be, the later Wittgenstein is no longer an *analytic* philosopher.

[1] It is noteworthy that Henri Bergson used this same metaphor to criticize the method of *analysis* in his *An Introduction to Metaphysics*.

CHAPTER VII

Meaning

The questioning of the existence of elementary propositions and the abandonment of the possibility of a final analysis meant nothing less than a complete repudiation of his earlier conception of language. The early Wittgenstein assumed that *the* function of language was to depict or 'picture' facts. According to this theory, words had their references and sentences had their senses. Combinations of linguistic elements corresponded to combinations of the elements of reality. Every proposition was built up from 'elementary propositions' which consist of names signifying simple objects. For it was assumed that ultimately the meaning of a word consists in what it *names*.

In the *Investigations* Wittgenstein came to realize that the doctrines of the *Tractatus* rested on a 'particular picture of the essence of human language'. It is the 'correspondence theory of meaning', the essence of which is this: the individual words in language name objects, the object for which a word stands is its meaning.[1] The greater part of the *Investigations* is directed against this conception of language (or what he calls the Augustinian conception of language).

[1] It follows from this theory that one group of words (such as 'apple', 'chair', and 'red') *name* objects in the 'external' world while another group of words (such as 'pain', 'pleasure', and 'belief') *name* objects in the 'internal' world. The problem of universals and the 'private language' problem are directly related to these two aspects of the correspondence theory of meaning. Wittgenstein's attack on essentialism and the private language can only be seen in the right light as the two-fronted attack on this particular conception.

St. Augustine assumed that the mastery of language consisted in learning the names of objects. This is a well-
established idea among traditional philosophers, including
the author of the *Tractatus*. Wittgenstein begins to criticize
this particular conception of language by first pointing out
that Augustine fails to recognize any difference between
kinds of words. If you describe the learning of language as
essentially a *naming* activity you are, Wittgenstein points
out, thinking primarily of nouns like 'table', 'chair', 'apple',
and of people's names, and only secondarily of the names of
certain sensations, actions and properties; but not of words
such as 'five', 'soon', 'or', and innumerable other kinds of
words.

Suppose, says Wittgenstein, that I send someone shopping
and give him a slip marked 'five red apples'. He takes it to
the shopkeeper, who goes to the box marked 'apples'; then
he looks up the word 'red' in a colour chart and finds a
colour sample beside it; then he recites the cardinal numbers
up to the word 'five' and for each number he takes an apple
of the same colour as the sample from the box. The test of
the shopkeeper's understanding of what is written on the
slip is that he *acts* as described. In this imaginary use of
language it makes sense to ask: 'What does the word "apple"
refer to?' and 'What does the word "red" refer to?' But what
if someone asks, 'What does the word "five" refer to?' This
question makes sense only if one assumes that the word
'five' has exactly the same kind of function as (or belongs to
the same category as) 'apples' and 'red'. That is to say, since
we can *point* to real objects (apples and colour samples) as
the references of 'apples' and 'red', we feel that there must
be something we can point to as the reference of 'five'. To
the question, 'What is the reference of the word "five"?'
Wittgenstein answers, 'No such thing was in question here,
only how the word "five" is used' (P.I. §1). The point
here is to reject the question.

In the above imaginary language situation, or what

Wittgenstein calls 'language-game', the *use* of the word 'five' is quite clear, the question as to the meaning of the word 'five' has no sense in that context. The urge to ask for the *meaning* of a word even when its *use* is perfectly clear arises from the 'philosophical concept of meaning' which 'has its place in a primitive idea of the way language functions' (P.I. §2). It is possible to imagine a language-game in which the primitive idea (or the Augustinian conception) of language would be right. Let's assume that the language is meant to serve for communication between a builder *A* and an assistant *B*. *A* is building with building-stones and *B* has to pass the stones in the order in which *A* needs them. For this purpose they use a language consisting of words 'block', 'pillar', 'slab', 'beam'. *A* calls them out,— *B* is trained to bring them when called. Augustine's conception of language as consisting of names would be an appropriate description of this particular system of communication;—only not everything that we call language is this system. It is, Wittgenstein points out, 'as if someone were to say: "A game consists in moving objects about on a surface according to certain rules . . ."—and we replied: You seem to be thinking of board games, but there are others' (P.I. §3).

Intimately connected with the Augustinian conception of language is the view that 'ostensive' definition is the fundamental act by which the meaning of a word is given. It is generally assumed that 'explanation of the meaning of a word' is roughly divided into verbal and ostensive definitions. The verbal definition, as it takes us from one verbal expression to another, in a sense gets us no further. Hence, all learning of the meaning ultimately depends on the ostensive definition,—it establishes a direct relationship between the meaning and the word.

Against this view, Wittgenstein points out, for one thing, that for many words in our language there do not seem to be ostensive definitions; e.g. for such words as 'number', 'not', 'yet', etc. (B.B. p. 1). It is true that in the builder's language-game an important part of the training will consist in the teacher's pointing to the objects, directing the assistant's attention to them, and at the same time uttering a word; e.g. 'slab'. This ostensive teaching of words can be said to establish an association between the word and the thing. But the ostensive teaching can help to bring this about '. . . only together with a particular training. With different training the same ostensive teaching of these words would have effected a quite different understanding' (P.I. §6). That is to say, ostensive definition can be understood only in context. In different contexts with different training the explanation of the word; e.g. 'tove' by pointing to a pencil and saying 'this is tove' may be interpreted to mean variously: 'This is a pencil', 'This is round', 'This is red', 'This is wood', 'This is hard', 'This is one', etc., etc. (B.B. p. 2). Ostensive definition can always be misunderstood, it presupposes context and training. 'So one might say: the ostensive definition explains the use—the meaning—of the word when the overall role of the word in language is clear' (P.I. §30).

Let us now look at an expansion of the builder's language. Besides the four words 'block', 'pillar', etc. let it contain the numerals, colour-names, and two other words 'there' and 'this'. The builder is now able to give his assistant more complicated orders such as: '5 red slabs there!' When the assistant learns this language, he has to learn the series of numerals 1, 2, 3, . . . by heart. Will this training include ostensive teaching?—Well, in a sense; people will, for example, point to slabs and count: '1, 2, 3 slabs'. Something more like the ostensive teaching of the words 'block', 'pillar', etc. would be the ostensive teaching of numerals that serve not to count but to refer to groups of objects that can be taken in at a glance.

How about 'there' and 'this?' Are they taught ostensively? If we stretched our imagination, we may say that it involves some ostensive teaching since one might teach their use by pointing to places and things. However, 'in this case the pointing occurs in the *use* of the words too and not merely in learning the use' (P.I. §9), because the gesture of pointing together with the object pointed at can be used *instead* of the word.[1]

Let us add two more words, 'now' and 'later' to the above language-game and train the assistant to carry out orders such as: 'Five red bricks there now!' A part of training the assistant may involve dragging him to perform his work when you want the bricks *now* and restraining him when you want them *later*. *Pointing* may not be involved in this training at all. Are we still inclined to insist that 'now' and 'later' are taught ostensively? 'Now what do the words of this language *signify*?—What is supposed to shew what they signify, if not the kind of use they have? And we have already described that. So we are asking for the expression "This word signifies *this*" to be made a part of the description. In other words the description ought to take the form "The word ... signifies ...". ... But assimilating the descriptions of the uses of words in this way cannot make the uses themselves any more like one another. For, as we see, they are absolutely unlike' (P.I. §10).

Compare, e.g. the way in which the word 'five' is used with the way in which the word 'slab' is used and then with the ways 'there' and 'now' are used within the language-game in question. The difference comes out clearly when we compare the different procedures with which their uses are taught and the various jobs which are performed by means of those words. It is precisely for this reason that we imagine and describe different language-games.

Wittgenstein starts the *Blue Book* with the question: 'What is the meaning of a word?' This question, like the questions 'What is time?', 'What is truth?', 'What is beauty', etc., produce in us a mental cramp. 'We feel that we can't point

[1] Cf. G. E. Moore, op. cit., p. 260.

to anything in reply to them and yet ought to point to something. (We are up against one of the great sources of philosophical bewilderment: a substantive makes us look for a thing that corresponds to it).' (B.B. p.1). The phrase 'the meaning of a word' exercises a certain spell which results in the idea that there must be a thing (either an object or a quality) corresponding to each noun and adjective, that this thing is the meaning of the word, and is named by it as an individual is named by a proper name. (Compare 'the meaning of a word' with 'the colour of a flower'). To break this spell Wittgenstein first suggested that instead of asking 'What's the meaning?' we should ask 'What's the explanation of meaning?' This replacement brings the question down to earth and helps to cure us of the temptation to look for some object which we might call 'the meaning' (B.B. p. 1). Later, at the Cambridge Moral Sciences Club, he made the famous recommendation: 'Don't ask for the meaning, ask for the use.'[1] One advantage of this slogan is that 'use' carries with it no suggestion of an object corresponding to a word. Another is that 'use' cannot be understood merely by looking at the word, it can only be understood in contexts—both linguistic and social. This is why Wittgenstein suggests that instead of comparing the relationship between the word and the meaning to that between the money and the cow that you can buy with it, we should compare it to the relationship between money and its use (P.I. §120). The use of money is not an object separable from the money, and the specific use of money to buy things (cf. the specific use of words to name things) is only a part of, and makes sense only in, a larger and much more complicated system (financial and social). Thus Wittgenstein provides this rule of thumb in the *Investigations*: 'For a *large* class of cases—though not for all—in which we employ the word "meaning" it can be explained thus: the meaning of a word is its use in the language' (P.I. §43).

[1] John Wisdom, 'Wittgenstein, 1934–27', in Fann (ed.) op. cit., p. 46.

Wittgenstein invites us to compare words in a language with tools in a tool-box. 'Think of words as instruments characterized by their use' (B.B. p. 67). 'Think of the tools in a tool-box: there is a hammer, pliers, a saw, a screw-driver, a rule, a glue-pot, glue, nails and screws.—The functions of words are as diverse as the functions of these objects' (P.I. §11). A word is characterized by its use just as a tool is characterized by its function. This analogy aptly reminds us that words are used for different purposes. There is not *one* function that all words have in common (e.g. to name things). The demand for a general theory of the meaning of words is quite pointless.[1] It is as if someone were to claim: '*all* tools serve to modify something. Thus the hammer modifies the position of the nail, the saw the shape of the board, and so on.' And what is modified by the rule?—'Our knowledge of a thing's length.' What about the glue-pot? Wittgenstein asks at this point: 'Would anything be gained by this assimilation of expressions?' (P.I. §14).

Sentences as well as words may be understood as tools or instruments. When we become confused about the sense of a sentence, Wittgenstein offers us the following advice: 'Look at the sentence as an instrument, and at its sense as its employment' (P.I. §421). 'Ask yourself: On what occasion, for what purpose, do we say this? What kind of actions accompany these words? (Think of the greeting). In what scenes will they be used; and what for?' (P.I. §489). It is in this way that we come to see how words and sentences are instruments used to accomplish certain purposes. Thus, in one of his private conversations, Wittgenstein said, 'To understand a sentence is to be prepared for one of its uses. If we can't think of any use for it at all, then we don't understand it at all'.[2] The use of language ordinarily has a

[1] He stated in one of his lectures that the idea of a general notion of meaning is in a way 'obsolete'. See Moore, op. cit., p. 258.
[2] See Malcolm, op. cit., p. 90.

point just as instruments are usually made for some purposes. But there is no single point of the practice of language as a whole. Wittgenstein lists a few of these purposes in the *Investigations*:

Giving orders, and obeying them—
Describing the appearance of an object, or giving its measurements—
Constructing an object from a description (a drawing)—
Reporting an event—
Speculating about an event—
Forming and testing a hypothesis—
Making up a story; and reading it—
Play-acting—
Singing catches—
Guessing riddles—
Making a joke; telling it—
Solving a problem in practical mathematics—
Translating from one language into another—
Asking, thanking, cursing, greeting, praying (P.I. 23)—

Immediately following this list Wittgenstein adds this significant remark: 'It is interesting to compare the multiplicity of the tools in language and of the ways they are used, the multiplicity of kinds of word and sentence, with what logicians have said about the structure of language. (Including the author of the *Tractatus Logico-Philosophicus*).' In this criticism of logicians and his former self, he is warning us against oversimplifying our concept of language. It is not one practice or one instrument, having one essential function and serving one essential purpose. Language is not one tool serving one purpose but a collection of tools serving a variety of purposes. 'Language is not defined for us as an arrangement fulfilling one definite purpose. Rather "language" is for us a name for a collection' (Z. §322).

What emerges from all these considerations is an instrumentalist (or pragmatic) conception of language. 'Language is an instrument. Its concepts are instruments' (P.I. §569). It is like a working machine which gets jobs done—namely everyday activities of life.

CHAPTER VIII

Language

In the previous chapter we directed our attention to the pragmatic nature of language. This was brought out by comparing a word with a tool and by describing the use of a word in a language-game. However, Wittgenstein was interested in reminding us of another important feature of language—i.e. its *social* nature. The point is made whenever he compares languages with games, or whenever he speaks of, and constructs different 'language-games'. Wittgenstein now invites us to compare language with a chess game and to look at a word as a piece in chess and an utterance with a move in chess. 'We are talking about the spatial and temporal phenomenon of language, not about some non-spatial, non-temporal phantasm. . . . But we talk about it as we do about the piece in chess when we are stating the rules of the game, not describing their physical properties. The question "What is a word really?" is analogous to "What is a piece in chess?" ' (P.I. §108).[1]

To understand what a piece in chess is one must understand the whole game, the rules defining it, and the role of the piece in the game. Similarly we might say, the meaning of a word is its place in a language-game. To put it in another way, the meaning of any single word in a language is 'defined', 'constituted', 'determined', or 'fixed' (he used all four expressions in different lectures) by the 'grammatical rules' with which it is used in that language.[2] Using a sen-

---

[1] This analogy appeared also in *Philosophische Bemerkungen* §18.
[2] See Moore, op. cit., p. 257.

tence is, thus, analogous to making a move in chess following the rules. Wittgenstein put it this way: '. . . a move in chess doesn't consist simply in moving a piece in such-and-such a way on the board . . . but in the circumstances that we call "playing a game of chess", "solving a chess problem", and so on' (P.I. §33). Such a move is comparable to making utterances in a language: 'Can I say "bububu" and mean "If it doesn't rain I shall go for a walk?". . . . It is only in language that I can mean something by something' (P.I. p. 18ᵉ note). Thus we cannot call anything a word or a sentence unless it is part of that kind of a rule-governed activity which we call a language. A language, we may say, is a set of activities (or practices) defined by certain rules, namely the rules which govern all the various uses of words in the language.

In order to be clear about the social nature of language Wittgenstein suggests that we ask ourselves: What is it for someone to follow a rule? What does the activity called 'following a rule' consist in? To start with, Wittgenstein asks, 'Is what we call 'following a rule" something that it would be possible for only *one* man to do, and to do only *once* in his life?' (P.I. §199).[1] The question is a conceptual one calling not for empirical investigation but a logical analysis of the concept of following a rule. Wittgenstein says that it is not possible (it doesn't make sense) that there should have been only one occasion on which someone followed a rule. Of course, we can imagine situations in which a new rule is followed by someone only once and then set aside. If such a case should arise, it would happen only because there already exist rules and the practice of following them. Wittgenstein is talking about the *practice* of following rules, not this or that particular rule. It is not possible

---

[1] There is an irregularity in Anscombe's translation of 'einer Regel folgen'. It is sometimes translated as 'following a rule', and other times as 'obeying a rule.' The first translation seems to me more appropriate and hence I shall consistently use 'following' in my quotations.

that only once in the history of man there was such a thing as following a rule. It is not possible that there should have been only one occasion on which an order was given, a promise made, a question asked, a debt procured, or a game played. Following a rule, making a promise, giving an order, and so on, are *customs, uses, practices,* or *institutions* (P.I. §199). They presuppose a society, a form of life.[1]

To understand rules it is necessary to understand the whole institution of 'following rules'. If the background of custom is removed, the rules embedded in this custom would also disappear. Wittgenstein shows this by the following example: 'What has the expression of a rule—say a sign-post—got to do with my actions? What sort of connexion is there here?—Well, perhaps this one: I have been trained to react to this sign in a particular way. . . . But that is only to give a causal connexion; to tell how it has come about that we now go by the sign-post; not what this going-by-the-sign really consists in. On the contrary; . . . a person goes by a sign-post only in so far as there exists a regular use of sign-posts, a custom' (P.I. §198).

In another context Wittgenstein asks, 'How does it come about that this arrow ⟫————————→ *points?* Doesn't it seem to carry in it something besides itself?' (P.I. §454). We might answer, 'No, not the dead line on the paper; only the psychical thing, the meaning, can do that.' Wittgenstein says that this answer is both true and false. It is true that the line in itself is totally dead; however, what makes it alive is not the 'psychical thing'. 'This pointing is not a hocus-pocus which can be performed only by the soul. The arrow points only in the application that a living being makes of it' (ibid.). This point is brought forcibly home by the following imaginary situation which Wittgenstein used in one of his lectures. Suppose the members of a savage tribe decorate

---

[1] 'Following the rule' is an activity which is involved in every important activity we human beings engage in. Hence the importance of understanding the concept of rule.

the walls of their caves by writing on them rows of Arabic numerals—and suppose that what they write is exactly what would be written by someone doing arithmetical calculations. They do it exactly right every time, but they never use it except for internal decoration—never use it in computing how much wood they need to build a hut or how much food they need for a feast, and so on. Would you say they were doing mathematics?[1]

Suppose no applications were made of the arrow. Would it still point? Suppose there were no regular use of sign-posts and no conventions as to how a sign-post is to be interpreted, each individual interpreted it in his own way. Would the sign-post still function as a guide?

An immediate consequence of the above analysis is that there cannot (logically) be 'private rules'. 'Following a rule' is a practice. 'And to *think* one is following a rule is not to follow a rule. Hence it is not possible to follow a rule "privately": otherwise thinking one was following a rule would be the same thing as following it' (P.I. §202). Rules are 'public', and consequently it must be *possible* for more than one person to learn to follow the rule.

Imagine someone using a line as a rule in the following way: He holds a pair of compasses, and carries one of its points along the line that is the 'rule', while the other one draws the line that follows the rule. And while he moves along the ruling line he alters the opening of the compasses, apparently with great precision, looking at the rule the whole time as if it determined what he did. And watching him we see no kind of regularity in this opening and shutting of the compasses. We cannot learn his way of following the line from it. Here perhaps one really would say: 'The original seems to *intimate* to him which way he is to go. But it is not a rule' (P.I. §237).

[1] D. A. T. Gasking and A. C. Jackson, 'Wittgenstein as a Teacher', in Fann (ed.), op. cit., p. 50.

Why is it not a rule? Because the notion of following a rule is logically inseparable from the notion of *making a mistake*. If it is possible to say of someone that he is following a rule, then one can ask whether he is doing it correctly or not. Otherwise there is no foothold in his behaviour for the notion of a rule to take a grip. There is then no sense in describing his behaviour as following a rule, since everything he does is as good as anything else he might do, whereas the point of the concept of a rule is that it should enable us to evaluate what is being done.

The possibility of 'making a mistake' is what distinguishes someone's merely manifesting a *regularity* in his behaviour and his following a rule. Only in the latter case does it make sense to ask, 'Is he doing it correctly?' The question means 'Is he following the rule or is he violating it?' To violate a rule is not merely to do something unusual or irregular, something which one does not ordinarily do in a given circumstance. It is to make a mistake, to be at fault, to be subject to criticism.

Let us consider what is involved in making a mistake. Wittgenstein contends that 'following a rule' involves what he calls 'agreement to go on in the same way'. We should like to say: someone is following a rule if he always acts in the same way on the same kind of occasion. But this, though correct, does not advance matters since it is only in terms of a given rule that the word 'same' acquires a definite sense. 'The use of the word "rule" and the use of the word "same" are interwoven' (P.I. §225). Similarly, one does not learn to follow a rule by first learning the use of the word 'agreement'. 'Rather, one learns the meaning of "agreement" by learning to follow a rule. If you want to understand what it means to "follow a rule", you have already to be able to follow a rule' (R.F.M. p. 184).

By the same token, we do not learn to follow a rule by first learning the words 'correct' and 'incorrect', or 'right' and 'wrong'. Rather, to participate in rule-governed activities *is*, in a certain way, to accept that there is a right and a wrong way of doing things. This is manifested in the process of teaching,—'The words "right" and "wrong" are used when giving instruction in proceeding according to a rule. (The word "right" makes the pupil go on, the word "wrong" holds him back)' (R.F.M. p. 184). What is right and wrong in a given case can never depend on one's own caprice. As Wittgenstein points out, 'One would like to say: whatever is going to seem right to me is right. And that only means that here we can't talk about "right" ' (P.I. §258). I cannot make words mean what I want them to mean; I can use them meaningfully only if other people can come to understand how I am using them. In other words, when it comes to following rules I must accept certain conventions. A mistake is a contravention of what is *established* as correct; as such, it must be recognizable. That is, if I make a mistake in, say, my use of a word, other people must be able to point it out to me.

Wittgenstein brought out another characteristic of a rule in the following way. He first asks us to imagine an unknown tribe which *seems* to employ a language. But then suppose that '. . . when we try to learn their language we find it impossible to do so. For there is no regular connexion between what they say, the sounds they make, and their actions. . . . There is not enough regularity for us to call it "language" ' (P.I. §207). The point here is that if it is impossible to *train* a person to *use* an alleged language we cannot say that it is a language. More generally, if there is to be a practice defined by rules, there must be some way of learning how to engage in the practice or follow the rules. Thus, Wittgenstein contrasts acting according to a rule with acting according to inspiration.

Let us imagine a rule intimating to me which way I am to follow it; that is, as my eye travels along the line, a voice within me says: "*This* way!"—What is the difference between this process of obeying a kind of inspiration and that of following a rule? For they are surely not the same. In the case of inspiration I *await* direction. I shall not be able to teach anyone else my 'technique' of following the line. Unless, indeed, I teach him some way of hearkening, some kind of receptivity. But then, of course, I cannot require him to follow the line in the same way as I do (P.I. §232).

What makes a rule capable of being learned (or taught) is the fact that following it implies a regularity of behaviour. If one acts in accordance with a rule, it must make sense to say, 'Here he is doing the *same* thing as he did before', and also to say, 'Here he is doing the *correct* thing, there he is not.' The rule specifies which acts will count as being the same as other acts, and which acts are to be counted as correct. Unless both factors are stated, it would not be possible to learn or to teach what it is to follow (and also to break) the rule. One would not be able to know whether, in a given set of circumstances, the act which one was doing was an act of the kind required or forbidden by the rule, or whether such an act was the correct thing to do.

To sum it up: *Learning* how to follow rules is gaining mastery of a technique; it is acquiring a skill. *Teaching* someone how to follow rules is training him in a technique; it is developing in him a skill. *Knowing how* to follow rules is having a skill; it is being able to engage in a practice. All of this is true of learning, teaching, or knowing a language, according to Wittgenstein. 'To understand a sentence means to understand a language. To understand a language means to be master of a technique' (P.I. §199). When we learn a language, however, we learn not only one technique but a whole complex set of techniques. To speak a language is not just to engage in one practice, but to engage in many different practices. One might say that a language is a composite practice made up of a number of practices. The multiplicity and variety of the practices which constitute our language are emphasized by Wittgenstein in the series of 'language-games' which he constructs in his later writings.

At this point Wittgenstein takes up 'the great question that lies behind all these considerations'.—For someone might object against him: 'You talk about all sorts of language-games, but have nowhere said what the essence of a language-game, and hence of language is: What is common to all these activities, and what makes them into language or parts of language. You let yourself off the very part of the investigation that once [in the *Tractatus*] gave you yourself most headache, the part about the *general form of propositions* and of language.'

To this challenge Wittgenstein admits readily that he has not stated the essence of language.—'Instead of producing something common to all that we call language, I am saying that these phenomena have no one thing in common which makes us use the same word for all,—but that they are *related* to one another in many different ways. And it is because of this relationship, or these relationships, that we call them all "languages" ' (P.I. §65). He tries to explain this by comparing the concept of a language with that of a game.

Consider for example the proceedings that we call 'games'. I mean board-games, card-games, ball-games, Olympic games, and so on. What is common to them all?—Don't say: 'There *must* be something common, or they would not be called "games", '—but *look and see* whether there is anything common to all.—For if you look at them you will not see something that is common to *all*, but similarities, relationships, and a whole series of them at that. To repeat: don't think, but look!—Look for example at board-games, with their multifarious relationships. Now pass to card-games; here you find many correspondences with the first group, but many common features drop out, and others appear. When we pass next to ball-games, much that is common is retained, but much is lost. . . . And we can go through the many, many other groups of games in the same way; can see how similarities crop up and disappear.

And the result of this examination is: we see a complicated network of similarities overlapping and criss-crossing; sometimes overall similarities, sometimes similarities of detail.

I can think of no better expression to characterize these similarities than 'family resemblances'; for the various resemblances between members of a family . . . overlap and criss-cross in the same way.—And I shall say: 'games' form a family (P.I. §66–7).

By the same token, various language-games have not *one* thing in common but they form a family. We can extend our concept of language by adding and inventing new language-games just as in spinning a thread we twist fibre on fibre. 'And the strength of the thread does not reside in the fact that some one fibre runs through its whole length, but in the overlapping of many fibres' (P.I. §67, also B.B. p. 87).

Someone may object here: 'In spite of Wittgenstein's disclaimer has he not in reality defined the essence of language when he said that language is like a set of social practices and a set of instruments?' But this is not the case. Wittgenstein only pointed out certain very general features ('overall similarities') in respect of which all languages resemble one another and which one is likely not to notice when philosophizing. There are many social practices and instruments which are not languages. What Wittgenstein denies is that there is one 'distinguishing' feature which makes these practices and instruments languages. It is very important to keep in mind that Wittgenstein did not have a 'philosophy' of language. G. E. Moore, reporting on Wittgenstein's lectures in 1930–33, emphasized that although Wittgenstein discussed certain very general questions about language at great length, he said 'more than once, that he did not discuss these questions because he thought that language was the subject-matter of philosophy. He did not think so. He discussed it only because he thought that particular philosophical errors or "troubles in our thought" were due to false analogies suggested by our actual use of expressions; and he emphasized that it was only necessary for him to discuss those points about language which ... have led, or are likely to lead, to definite philosophical puzzles or errors.'[1]

[1] Moore, op. cit., p. 257 and p. 324.

CHAPTER IX

Philosophy

Wittgenstein's later view of language is indeed the antithesis of his earlier doctrine. Most characteristic of the later work is its opposition to what he considers the preoccupation of philosophers with linguistic form as distinct from function. Language is no longer looked at through what Ryle calls 'the slots of a logician's stencil' as a highly ordered system, but accepted in all its multiplicity and complexity. The eternal striving for absolute exactness and precision is now regarded as illusion—and vagueness, in so far as it serves our ordinary purposes, is accepted as reality. Instead of looking for the unifying principles, which obscure details and lead to abstracting of essences, he would draw our attention to case after case of real or imaginary 'uses' of language. The introduction of the 'language-game' in the virtually jargon-free later writings is precisely to bring out the oft forgotten fact that language has multiple functions and that words and expressions have meaning only in social contexts or in 'the stream of life'.[1]

The sharp contrast between the early and the later views of language, however, should not distract us from seeing the *point* of his 'critique of language'. His great concern in both periods has been the master problem: What are the nature, tasks, and methods of philosophy? He is not interested in language for language's sake but for the sake of philosophy. The specific area of traditional philosophy which catches and fixes his attention is his battleground. His

[1] Malcolm, op. cit., p. 93.

investigation, as he emphasized, 'gets its light, that is to say its purpose, from the philosophical problems' (P.I. §109). In the *Investigations*, just as in the *Tractatus*, Wittgenstein's task is to question the questions, to mark out the limits of sense, to indicate what can be said and what cannot be said. The limit, as he realized in the *Tractatus*, can only be set in language. To be sure, the boundary is drawn differently for different reasons in the two books. Still, to draw the boundary is Wittgenstein's major task in both.

This is made quite clear when Wittgenstein says, in the *Investigations*, that in a sense 'we too in these investigations are trying to understand the essence of language—its function, its structures', except that 'essence' here should be understood in an entirely different sense. For the early Wittgenstein sees in the essence, 'not something that already lies open to view and that becomes surveyable by a rearrangement, but something that lies *beneath* the surface. Something that lies within, which we see when we look *into* the thing, and which an analysis digs out' (P.I. §92). 'The book deals with the problems of philosophy, and shows, I believe, that the reason why these problems are posed is that the logic of our language is misunderstood.' This statement, from the preface of the *Tractatus*, could be a very appropriate summary of the *Investigations*.

The early Wittgenstein believed that he had discovered *the* essence of language, and revealed *the* limit of language. The boundary between sense and nonsense was set once and for all according to a definite criterion of meaning. The later Wittgenstein, however, no longer speaks of *the* language but of different uses of language or language-games. Consequently, there is no such thing as '*the* limit of language' but only 'limits of language' (P.I. §119). And there are no absolute criteria of 'sense' or 'nonsense',—'Where we say "This makes no sense" we always mean "This makes nonsense *in this particular* [language-]*game*".'[1] In fact, Wittgenstein

[1] Moore, op. cit., p. 273.

went as far as to state that ' "make sense" is vague, and will have different senses in different cases, but . . . the expression "make sense" is useful just as "game" is useful, although, like "game", it alters its meaning as we go from proposition to proposition.'[1] Thus, the criticism of an assertion as meaningless would always be a specific *ad hoc* argument relating to a context.

It is for this reason that Wittgenstein constructs various language-games in the process of criticizing specific metaphysical utterances. To make sure that his investigations are not construed as constituting a 'philosophy' of language, he explains: 'Our clear and simple language-games are not preparatory studies for a future regularization of language. . . . [They] are rather set up as *objects of comparison* which are meant to throw light on the facts of our language by way not only of similarities, but also of disimilarities' (P.I. §130). It is true that, with respect to treating specific philosophical problems, Wittgenstein's main concern is to draw our attention to the dissimilarities between different language-games in which the relevant words occur. Nevertheless, he wishes to remind us of certain over-all similarities among the language-games. 'We want to establish an order in our knowledge of the use of language: an order with a particular end in view; one out of many possible orders; not *the* order' (P.I. §132).[2] In the *Investigations*, Wittgenstein established an order in our knowledge of the use of language,—i.e. the pragmatic or instrumentalist conception of language, with a particular end in view—that of solving, or rather, *dis*solving

[1] Ibid., p. 274.
[2] Compare: P.I. §17, 'But how we group words into kinds will depend on the aim of the classification,—and on our inclination. Think of the different points of view from which one can classify tools or chessmen.'—For example, from the point of view of function, shape, material, colour, weight, etc. Wittgenstein is interested in grouping words according to their *functions* just as we usually group tools according to the jobs they perform and chessmen according to the roles they play in a game—hence, the invitation to look at words as tools or chess-men.

philosophical problems.[1] Although Wittgenstein now realizes that 'sense' and 'nonsense' are vague terms in ordinary language, nevertheless it is possible to *draw* a boundary according to the established order for a particular purpose. This is done in the *Investigations* when Wittgenstein advises us to look at the ordinary uses of language as a machine doing work. We may say that the general criteria by which the later Wittgenstein judges philosophical utterances to be nonsensical is the pragmatic criterion of meaning. This is shown by his submitting philosophical statements to questions such as: 'What use can we make of that statement?' 'What practical consequences is it supposed to have?' 'Under what circumstances, to achieve what, would you say that?' and so on. In the *Tractatus* the boundary was *discovered*, but in the *Investigations* the boundary is *drawn*.[2]

> To say 'This combination of words makes no sense' excludes it from the sphere of language and thereby bounds the domain of language. But when one draws a boundary it may be for various kinds of reason. If I surround an area with a fence or a line or otherwise, the purpose may be to prevent someone from getting in or out; but it may also be part of a game and the players be supposed, say, to jump over the boundary [metaphysical language-game?]; or it may shew where the property of one man ends and that of another begins [boundaries between science, metaphysics and religion, for example]; and so on. So if I draw a boundary line that is not yet to say what I am drawing it for (P.I. §499).

This important and often misunderstood passage throws

---

[1] This is made clear by the statement in the paragraph following the one just quoted: 'The clarity that we are aiming at is indeed *complete* clarity. But this simply means that the philosophical problems should *completely* disappear' (P.I. §133).

[2] Cf. 'Our investigation does not try to *find* the real, exact meaning of words; though we do often *give* words exact meanings in the course of our investigation' (Z. §467).

much light on Wittgenstein's later philosophy. Just as the *Tractatus* was misinterpreted as basically anti-metaphysical, the *Investigations* is now generally regarded as anti-metaphysical. This is largely due to his branding metaphysical statements as nonsensical in both books. However, the purpose of his *drawing* a boundary between sense and nonsense is not correctly understood. He is not attempting to eliminate metaphysics or to *end* all philosophy; his task is to *understand* their nature. I hope this point will become clearer further on. It may be noted here that Wittgenstein had a certain sympathy for metaphysical philosophers and that he told one of his students: 'Don't think I despise metaphysics or ridicule it. On the contrary, I regard the great metaphysical writings of the past as among the noblest productions of the human mind.'[1]

In Part I Wittgenstein's views on philosophy were seen to be the logical consequences of his theory of language. Similarly, his later conception of philosophy follows from his new way of looking at language.[2] It should not be difficult now to understand his 'diagnosis' and 'treatment' of the philosophical problems. Philosophical problems arise mainly through a misinterpretation of our forms of language,—they are 'linguistic' or rather 'conceptual' problems. That is not to say, however, that they are silly or unimportant problems.—They '. . . have the character of *depth*. They are deep disquietudes; their roots are as deep in us as the forms of our language and their significance is as great as the importance of our language' (P.I. §111).

For Wittgenstein, then, philosophy begins with puzzlement. Philosophical questions are tormenting questions arising from our forms of language; they are 'vexations' or 'intellectual discomfort' comparable to some kind of mental

---

[1] M. Drury, 'A Symposium on Wittgenstein', in Fann (ed.), op. cit., p. 68 and Cf. p. 126.

[2] His most important remarks about philosophy (P.I. §109–133) come right after his criticisms of his old theory of language.

disease. In a lecture, Wittgenstein said that philosophers were 'in a muddle about things'; that they follow a certain instinct which leads them to ask certain questions without understanding what those questions mean; that the asking of those questions results from 'a vague mental uneasiness', like that which leads children to ask 'Why?'[1] Hence, 'A philosophical problem has the form: "I don't know my way about" (P.I. §123). Elsewhere, a philosophical problem is compared to a 'mental cramp' to be relieved or a 'knot in our thinking' to be untied (Z. §452). And a person caught in a philosophical perplexity is compared to a man in a room who wants to get out but doesn't know how,[2] or a fly caught in a fly-bottle. Philosophy, as Wittgenstein conceives it, is thus 'a battle against the bewitchment of our intelligence by means of language' (P.I. §109). His aim is—'To show the fly the way out of the fly-bottle' (P.I. §309).

The metaphorical description of philosophical problems in psychological terms—such as 'mental cramp', 'mental torment', etc.,—is not accidental. For one thing, it is an expression of Wittgenstein's *personal* involvement with them. For another, it is an appropriate characterization of Wittgenstein's own methods and aim of philosophy. 'The philosopher's treatment of a question is like the treatment of an illness' (P.I. §255). Just as there is not *one* conclusive therapy for all mental illness; 'There is not *a* philosophical method, though there are indeed methods, like different therapies' (P.I. §133). Which therapy should be used would depend on the illness and the person who is afflicted by it. Nevertheless, like psychotherapy, the first step is to look round for the *source* of the philosophical puzzlement (B.B. p. 59). For example, if a patient is suffering from delusions, it would not be of any help to tell him that he is merely having delusions. To cure him an analyst must seek out the cause of his illness. Similarly, Wittgenstein points out,

[1] Moore, op. cit., p. 323.
[2] Malcolm, op. cit., p. 51.

'When the solipsist says that only his own experiences are real, it is no use answering him: "Why do you tell us this if you don't believe that we really hear it?" Or anyhow, if we give him this answer, we mustn't believe that we have answered his difficulty. <u>There is no common sense answer to a philosophical problem.</u> One can defend common sense against the attacks of philosophers only by solving their puzzles, i.e. by curing them of the temptation to attack common sense; not by restating the views of common sense' (B.B. pp. 58–9).[1] We must try to understand *why* the metaphysicians want to make such paradoxical statements. Wittgenstein's philosophical therapy is analogous to psychotherapy in another respect. The goal in both cases is to get rid of the illness. 'The real discovery is the one that makes me capable of stopping doing philosophy when I want to.— The one that gives philosophy peace, so that it is no longer tormented by questions which bring *itself* in question' (P.I. §133). In a sense, he is exactly where he started; for philosophy <u>'leaves everything as it is'</u> (P.I. §124). However, philosophy is never trivial or unimportant just as treatment by psycho-analysis should not be regarded as trivial on the ground that it merely restores a man's sanity.

In describing Wittgenstein's criticisms of his own earlier theories of meaning and language we have already pointed out what he considered to be traditional philosophers' mistakes and have demonstrated his methods of dealing with those problems. Nevertheless, we shall attempt to summarize some of his more general criticisms of traditional philosophy and also to illustrate his new methods by specific examples. <u>The main mistake made by philosophers</u> (in-

---

[1] Wittgenstein is, no doubt, attacking G. E. Moore here. In his notes *On Certainty*, Wittgenstein criticizes Moore's 'A Defence of Common Sense' along this line. Moore's contribution to philosophy lies in detecting the oddness of metaphysical claims but his mistake lies in trying to counter metaphysical statements (e.g. 'We cannot prove the existence of an external world') by statements of common sense (e.g. 'Here is one hand, . . . and here is another.')

cluding the author of the *Tractatus*), according to Wittgenstein, is that 'When language is looked at, what is looked at
is a form of words and not the use made of the form of
words'.[1] When we are doing philosophy we are confused
by the uniform appearance of words when we hear them
spoken or meet them in script and print. But their *application*
is not presented to us clearly. It is like looking into the cabin
of a locomotive. We see handles all looking more or less
alike. Traditional philosophy, we may say, is concerned
with handles. It treats of terms, words as handles; it
ignores to a large extent the different ways the handles
work. 'We remain unconscious of the prodigious diversity
of all the everyday language-games because the clothing of
our language makes everything alike' (P.I. p. 224). This is
a very important point which Wittgenstein wants to remind
us of over and over again in the *Investigations*. He distinguishes the 'surface-grammar' from the 'depth-grammar' in
the use of words. The 'surface-grammar' is 'What immediately impresses itself upon us about the use of a word . . .,
the part of its use—one might say—that can be taken in by
the ear' (P.I. §664). The 'depth-grammar', then, is the
application of words.

A few examples here would help to clarify the distinction.
Compare the propositions: 'I have a beautiful hat' and 'I
have a terrible toothache'. The similarity in their surface-
grammar is obvious but their *uses* are quite different (cf.
B.B. p. 53). The difference in their depth-grammar may be
brought out by comparing, e.g. 'Is this my hat?' and 'Is this
my toothache?'—(nonsense). Compare again: 'All roses
have thorns' and 'All rods have length'. On the surface, both
propositions seem to be empirical generalizations, but while
we can imagine roses without thorns, can we also imagine
rods without length? How do we decide whether all rods
have length? Do we examine rods as we would examine

---

[1] *Lectures and Conversations* (Oxford, 1966), p. 2.

roses? The second proposition is not experiential but logical or, as Wittgenstein calls it, 'grammatical'; it does not give us information about rods but states a rule governing the use of the word 'rod'.

We all know what 'It is 5 o'clock here' means; do we also know what 'It is 5 o'clock on the sun' means? What is the criterion for application here? Don't we understand this statement: 'Although the deaf-mutes have learned only a gesture-language, each of them really talks to himself inwardly in a vocal language'? Wittgenstein remarks: 'What can I do with this information (if it is such)? The whole idea of understanding smells fishy here. I do not know whether I am to say I understand it or don't understand it. I might answer: "It's an English sentence; *apparently* [the surface-grammar] quite in order—that is until one wants to do something with it; . . ."' (P.I. §348).

Let us look at another example. 'The Earth has existed for millions of years' makes clearer sense than 'The Earth has existed only in the last five minutes', or 'The Earth has just sprung into being now'. We know the ideas and observations associated with the former proposition but what observations do the latter propositions refer to, and what observations would count against them? (P.I. p. 221).[1] Compare the following sentences: 'A newborn child has no teeth.'—'A goose has no teeth.'—'A rose has no teeth.' 'This last at any rate—one would like to say—is obviously true! It is even surer than that a goose has none. —And yet it is none so clear. For where should a rose's teeth have been?' (P.I. p. 221).

In every case '. . . there is a picture in the foreground [the surface-grammar] but the sense lies far in the background; that is, the application of the picture [the depth-grammar] is not easy to survey' (P.I. §422). The picture is *there*; and

---

[1] This is a criticism of Russell's statement in *The Problems of Philosophy* that it is logically possible that the world might have sprung into being 5 minutes ago. See Moore, op. cit., p. 320.

Wittgenstein does not dispute its correctness. But *what* is its application? The 'pragmatism' in Wittgenstein's later philosophy is becoming more and more pronounced.[1] 'One might say: the axis of reference of our examination must be rotated, but about the fixed point of our real need' (P.I. §108). Instead of concentrating on the theoretical study of linguistic forms (as he did in the *Tractatus*), he is now concerned with the pragmatic examination of linguistic functions. A boundary of sense is *drawn* around the criteria of 'use', 'purpose', 'employment', 'practical consequence', etc. The purpose of drawing this boundary is to remind ourselves that 'It is not every sentence-like formation that we know how to do something with, not every technique has an application in our life; and when we are tempted in philosophy to count some quite useless thing as a proposition, that is often because we have not considered its application sufficiently' (P.I. §520). 'The confusions which occupy us arise when language is like an engine idling, not when it is doing work' (P.I. §132). 'Philosophical problems arise when language *goes on holiday*' (P.I. §38).

A metaphysical pronouncement is like '. . . a wheel that can be turned though nothing else moves with it, [it] is not part of the mechanism' (P.I. §271). Its main cause is precisely due to the difficulty in understanding the 'depth-grammar' of some sentences. The form of a metaphysical utterance makes it look like an empirical proposition but it is really a 'grammatical' or conceptual one.[2] As Wittgenstein puts it, 'The essential thing about metaphysics: it obliterates the distinction between factual and conceptual investigation' (Z. §458). Compare:

[1] He refers to pragmatism a number of times in his lectures. In his last notes *On Certainty* we find entries such as: 'In other words I want to say something that sounds like pragmatism. A kind of Weltanschauung cuts across my path.'

[2] Wittgenstein seems to use 'grammatical', 'conceptual', and sometimes 'logical' or 'tautological' interchangeably. Also: 'empirical', 'experiential', and 'factual' are used interchangeably.

(1) Only one person can play patience.

(2) Only one person can sit on a bench 6 inches wide.

(3) Only one person can feel my pain.

The 'surface-grammar' is quite alike, but their 'depth-grammar' is utterly different. (2) states a physical impossibility and (1) states a 'grammatical' impossibility—it makes no sense to speak of playing patience with another person. (3) has an experiential form;—a philosopher who says this may well think that he is expressing a kind of scientific truth. However, can we imagine its opposite? What would it be like for someone else to feel my pain? When we say 'One man cannot feel another's pain', the idea of an insurmountable physical barrier suggests itself to us, while the impossibility is really logical.—It states a grammatical rule governing the use of the word 'pain', much in the same way that (1) states a grammatical rule (cf. P.I. §248 and B.B. p. 56).

What Wittgenstein always does when he meets the word 'can' in a metaphysical proposition is to show 'that this proposition hides a grammatical rule. That is to say, we destroy the outward similarity between a metaphysical proposition and an experiential one' (B.B. p. 55). Propositions such as 'Every rod has length', 'Sensations are private', 'Time has only one direction', etc. are 'A full-blown pictorial representation of our grammar' (P.I. §295). To free us from the misleading forms of metaphysical expressions, Wittgenstein suggests that instead of saying 'one cannot . . .', we say 'there is no such thing as . . . in this game'. 'Not: "One can't castle in draughts" but—"there is no castling in draughts"; and instead of "I can't exhibit my sensation"—"in the use of the word 'sensation', there is no such thing as exhibiting what one has got"; instead of "one cannot enumerate all the cardinal numbers"—"there is no such thing as enumerating all the numbers" ' (Z. §134).

'Grammar tells what kind of object anything is' (P.I.

§373)—It expresses the *essence* of a thing (P.I. §371, cf. R.F.M. I, §32, §105). If someone says, 'This body has extension', we might reply: 'Nonsense!'—but are inclined to say 'Of course!'—Why is this? (P.I. §252). We are inclined to reply the latter because, in a sense, it contains so much truth—so much that we cannot imagine its negation (cf. Z. §460). Nevertheless, we might want to say 'Nonsense! Who are you informing? You speak as if it is an experiential statement!' When Wittgenstein says, as he often does in his later writings, that metaphysical propositions are 'nonsense', 'senseless', or 'without sense',[1] we should keep in mind the distinction he wishes to make:—'Nonsense is produced by trying to express by the use of language what ought to be embodied in the grammar'.[2] Wittgenstein explained in his lectures that it was in this particular sense that he thought both the Realist and the Idealist were 'talking nonsense'.[3] Compare this with the formulation in the *Tractatus*: Nonsense is produced by attempting to *say* what cannot be said. The parallel between his earlier and later views of metaphysics is obvious. As in the *Tractatus*, Wittgenstein opposes the typical metaphysical *way* of expressing certain 'fundamental things' in the empirical form (Z. §459). If we therefore, think Wittgenstein is against metaphysics *per se*, we should remember his remarks about poetry: 'Do not forget that a poem, even though it is composed in the language of information, is not used in the language-game of giving information' (Z. §160).

Since this aspect of Wittgenstein's later philosophy is often misunderstood, I shall attempt to clarify it in another way. Wittgenstein often draws the analogy between language

[1] He does not distinguish these terms in the *Investigations* as he did in the *Tractatus*.

[2] Moore, op. cit., p. 312.

[3] Ibid. p. 311, Cf. 'The Solipsists' statement "Only my experience is real" is absurd "as a statement of fact". . . . Solipsism is right if it merely says that "I have toothache" and "he has toothache" are on quite a different level.'

and the chess-game, and different uses of language are compared to different moves in a game. Learning the initial positions of each chessman and the rules defining each piece, etc., is not yet 'playing' the game, but *preparing* to play. Similarly, grammatical propositions are '*preparations* for the use of language, almost like definitions are. . . . [They] are part of the *apparatus* of language, not of the *application* of language.'[1] If the applications of language are compared to different houses serving different purposes (cf. P.I. §18), then the *apparatus* of language is comparable to the ground on which the houses stand. 'Where does our investigation get its importance from, since it seems only to destroy everything interesting, that is, all that is great and important? . . . But we are only destroying castles-in-the-air, and we are laying open the ground of language on which they stood' (P.I. §118).[2] Different language-games are like houses which are built for different purposes. A metaphysical proposition is, as it were, a pretence use of language. Metaphysics pretends to be a kind of science. In this respect, Wittgenstein continues to adhere to his earlier insight: 'Philosophy is not one of the natural sciences' (T. 4.111). This is reaffirmed in the *Investigations*: 'It was true to say that our considerations could not be scientific ones' (P.I. §109). He criticizes metaphysics because it has been *presented* in an empirical form, not because it deals with unimportant matters. When he criticizes Freud, for example: 'Freud is constantly claiming to be scientific. But what he gives is *speculation*—something prior even to the formation of an hypothesis'[3], it is not because he thinks that Freud was doing something unimportant. He is merely warning us not to take Freud's words at their face value, but to look at them in a different light. Metaphysics deals with very funda-

---

[1] *Wittgenstein's Lectures in the Spring of 1939*, lecture notes taken by Norman Malcolm (unpublished), p. 89.

[2] My translation.

[3] *Lectures and Conversations*, p. 44.

mental matters—it is concerned with the *ground* of language, and consequently, of reality.[1]

Wittgenstein conceives his philosophical task to be helping those who are philosophically puzzled to see the nature of their puzzlement. It is true that he tends to emphasize the negative aspects of philosophy. But we might remember the following parable Wittgenstein used to explain the verification principle: Imagine that there is a town where the policemen are required to obtain information about the kind of work each inhabitant does. Occasionally, a policeman comes across someone who does not do *any* work. The policeman enters this fact on the record, because *this too* is a useful piece of information about the man![2] The moral of this parable is that if we discover a proposition to be unverifiable, then that is an important piece of information about it. Thus, he says: 'Asking whether and how a proposition can be verified is only a particular way of asking "How d'you mean?" The answer is a contribution to the grammar of the proposition' (P.I. §353).

Wittgenstein suggested some positive ways of looking at metaphysics. He emphasized that although metaphysical statements, taken at their face value, are absurd; the 'idea expressed by them is of enormous importance.'—They exhibit clearly the grammar of certain important words in our language. Our ordinary language 'holds our mind rigidly in one position, as it were, and in this position sometimes it feels cramped, having a desire for other positions as well' (B.B. p. 59). A metaphysician invents a notation which stresses a difference more strongly, makes it more obvious than ordinary language does. In a sense he has discovered 'a new way of looking at things. As if [he] had invented a new way of painting; or, again, a new metre, or a new kind of song' (P.I. §401).—All of these require

---

[1] 'Our investigation . . . is directed not towards phenomena, but, as one might say, towards the "*possibilities*" of phenomena' (P.I. §89–90).

[2] Malcolm, op. cit., p. 66.

great talent and insight. No wonder he regarded 'the great metaphysical writings of the past as among the noblest productions of the human mind'.

Wittgenstein's later work, as we have seen, is not anti-metaphysical; although it is non-metaphysical. His main task is to *understand* the nature of metaphysics and his contribution, above all, lies in suggesting a new way of looking at philosophy. Nevertheless, we may benefit from pondering over a remark by one of his close friends: 'The whole driving force of [Wittgenstein's] investigation is missed if it is not seen continually to point beyond itself.'[1]

[1] Drury, 'A Symposium', in Fann (ed.), op. cit., p. 70.

CHAPTER X

Understanding Wittgenstein

Because of the novel nature of his philosophy and the aphoristic and cryptic style of his writings, Wittgenstein's work lends itself readily to all sorts of interpretations and misinterpretations. In this chapter I shall examine some of the major criticisms levelled against Wittgenstein and suggest a way of looking at his work which would avoid certain misinterpretations.

Many of Wittgenstein's statements are vague and, as he pointed out, are sometimes *meant* to be vague (B.B. p. 84). His most important insights are expressed in analogies, metaphors and parables;—because of the extreme difficulty of the subject matter. (He is, in a sense, still trying to say what cannot be said.) Nevertheless, this does not mean he can be interpreted in whatever fashion one wishes. It is not uncommon for some of Wittgenstein's remarks to be understood in exactly the opposite way to what was intended. For example, it is apparently possible for a philosopher to interpret Wittgenstein thus: 'Old-style philosophy for him teaches nothing, changes nothing, "it leaves everything as it is".'[1] And Wittgenstein's later view of language is understood by another philosopher to be thus: 'The language-game is also a logic game. Here Wittgenstein is advancing a thesis not too far removed from the viewpoint of Hilbert: "if anyone utters a sentence and *means* or *understands* it he is operating a calculus according to definite rules"' (P.I. §81).[2]

[1] Leslie Paul, *Persons and Perception* (London, 1961), p. 42.
[2] James Feibleman, *Inside the Great Mirror* (The Hague, 1958), p.

These kinds of misinterpretations are not serious, as they are so obvious. However, there are many serious criticisms which require our analysis. We have seen that Wittgenstein is not anti-metaphysical (Ch. IX), not an 'analytic' philosopher (Ch. VI), and not a 'common-sense' philosopher (Ch. IX). Is he an 'ordinary-language' philosopher? Has he 'explicitly laid it down that our ordinary expressions are "in order as they are"', and has forbidden philosophers to tamper with them?' Is it true that 'His own system makes no provision for the adoption of any new way of speaking in conflict with existing practice', as David Pole has claimed?[1] And what about Cornforth's accusation: 'When Wittgenstein set up the actual use of language as a standard, that was equivalent to accepting a certain set-up of culture and belief as a standard. . . . It is lucky no such philosophy was thought of until recently or we should still be under the sway of witch doctors. . . .'[2] A long quotation from the *Blue Book* here will help to dispel the kind of misunderstanding revealed by these criticisms.

A philosopher is not a man out of his sense, a man who doesn't see what everybody sees; nor on the other hand is his disagreement with common sense that of the scientist disagreeing with the coarse views of the man in the street. That is, his disagreement is not founded on a more subtle knowledge of fact. We therefore have to look round for the source of his puzzlement. . . .

Now the man whom we call a solipsist and who says that only his own experiences are real, does not thereby dis-

[1] David Pole, *The Later Philosophy of Wittgenstein* (London, 1958), p. 79.
[2] Maurice Cornforth, *Marxism and the Linguistic Philosophy* (New York, 1965), p. 163.

---

206. He failed to quote the first half of the sentence which makes Wittgenstein's sense clear: 'For it will then also become clear what can lead us (and did lead me [obviously referring to the *Tractatus*]) to think that if anyone utters a sentence and . . .'.

agree with us about any practical question of fact, he does not say that we are simulating when we complain of pains, he pities us as much as anyone else, and at the same time he wishes to restrict the use of the epithet 'real' to what we should call his experiences; ... And why shouldn't we grant him this notation? I needn't say that in order to avoid confusion he had in this case better not use the word 'real' as opposed to 'simulated' at all; ... (B.B. p. 59).

Philosophy is not science. The philosopher is neither a theoretical scientist who gives us explanatory theories, nor an empirical scientist who discovers new facts. 'Philosophy simply puts everything before us, and neither explains nor deduces anything.—Since everything lies open to view there is nothing to explain. For what is hidden, for example, is of no interest to us' (P.I. §126). Don't forget that Wittgenstein is dealing with 'philosophical' problems—'The concepts of meaning, of understanding, of a proposition, of logic, the foundations of mathematics, states of consciousness, and other things' (P.I. Preface). A philosophical problem is like a jig-saw puzzle,—all the pieces (facts) are there, only all mixed up (B.B. p. 46). There is nothing *hidden* in philosophical problems. What is hidden is of no interest to us *as* philosophers, although it may well be of great interest to scientists. Philosophers' disagreement with common sense is not about electrons, neurons, magnetic fields, etc., but, so to speak, about tables, chairs, and things everybody is familiar with. It is in this context that Wittgenstein says: 'When philosophers use a word—"knowledge", "being", "object", "I", "proposition", "name"—and try to grasp the *essence* of the thing, one must always ask oneself: is the word ever actually used in this way in the language[1] which is its original home?—What *we* do is to bring words

[1] In the original, Wittgenstein speaks of 'der Sprache' and not 'der Sprachspiel'. Anscombe mistakenly translates it as 'language-game' in the English text.

back from their metaphysical to their everyday use' (P.I.
§116).

It is only *when* philosophers use words in the metaphysical
way that we bring them back to their everyday use.[1] (Compare: '. . . whenever someone else wanted to say something
metaphysical, [we] demonstrate to him that he had failed
to give a meaning to certain signs in his propositions.'—T.
6.53). This characterizes Wittgenstein's method—to remind
the philosopher who says 'only my experiences are real' that
he is not using the word 'real' in any ordinary sense as
when we use it in contrast with 'simulated', etc. For this
reason Wittgenstein used to ask: 'What would my bed-
maker say of this kind of abstract talk?' when he was faced
with metaphysical statements such as: 'We don't really
know that the external world exists', 'The bed is *really* a
bundle of sense-data', 'The existence of other minds is only a
hypothesis', and so on. It was in this sort of situation that
Wittgenstein said 'What the bed-maker says is all right, but
what (the metaphysicians) say is all wrong'.[2] Does this mean
that he now advocates the 'bed-maker's' world view and her
language as a standard?

Pole says, or implies, that Wittgenstein regards ordinary
language as 'sacrosanct', and that he speaks in the name of
nothing higher than the 'status quo'. Thus he complains:
'Wittgenstein's whole treatment of language takes no
account of the necessity or possibility of its growth, . . . it
comes near to prohibiting it.'[3] And Cornforth contends that
'When [Wittgenstein] said that philosophy "may not
interfere", that came to saying that it may not interfere with
currently accepted culture and belief.'[4] These accusations

---

[1] This includes everyday use of language by scientists, artists, mathe-
maticians, neuro-surgeons, etc.

[2] See W. Mays, 'Recollections of Wittgenstein', in Fann (ed.), op. cit.,
p. 82 and p. 338.

[3] Pole, op. cit., p. 92.

[4] Cornforth, loc. cit.

arise from Wittgenstein's statement: 'Philosophy may in no way interfere with the actual use of language; it can in the end only describe it' (P.I. §124). For Pole and Cornforth this statement meant either that philosophy ought not to change it or that the actual use of language may in no way be changed. What the statement means is that philosophy (as Wittgenstein conceives it) does not change it, although of course there are many ways of changing ordinary language—and it in fact changes constantly. Wittgenstein makes this quite clear in the following passages:

> [The multiplicity of language] is not something fixed, given once for all; but new types of language, new language-games, as we may say, come into existence, and others become obsolete and get forgotten (P.I. §23).

> ... a reform [of ordinary language] for particular practical purposes, an improvement in our terminology designed to prevent misunderstandings in practice, is perfectly possible. But these are not the cases we have to do with (P.I. §132).

To Pole's accusation: '[Wittgenstein's] own system makes no provision for the adoption of any new way of speaking in conflict with existing practice', we might answer: 'It is quite true that Wittgenstein makes no provision for any new way of speaking, but he does not make any provision against it either, for he has no *system*.' It should be quite obvious that there is no 'system' in Wittgenstein's later philosophy.[1] Related to this is another kind of misunderstanding—viz. that Wittgenstein advances *theories* (of meaning, language, and what not) in the *Investigations*.

Pitcher asserts that in spite of Wittgenstein's explicit denial, 'He himself most certainly puts forward theses with which not everyone would agree.' One such 'thesis' is that

---

[1] It has been reported that once Wittgenstein flew at one of his students for suggesting that he was a 'systematic philosopher'.

'the meaning of an expression is its use in the language'.[1] He claims that Wittgenstein 'identifies the meaning of a word—and the sense of a sentence—with its use in the language'; and sets about to 'argue that this identification is mistaken'; and *then* tries to assure us that Wittgenstein's mistake does not really affect his valuable practice. Pitcher's curious argument is worth quoting at length here:

> Wittgenstein seems to have been laboring under the traditional assumption—perhaps a hold-over from the *Tractatus*—that it is the job of the philosopher to give us the real meaning of certain important words: and he is telling us that this meaning is neither the object(s), if any, denoted by the word nor any kind of spiritual atmosphere surrounding the word, but that it is rather the use(s) of the word in the language. What he might better have said, I think, is that it is not the job of the philosopher to give us the meaning of philosophically difficult words, but rather to give us their uses. As Wisdom put it, 'Don't ask for meaning, ask for the use,'[2] And this is actually what Wittgenstein himself does in practice: he investigates the uses of words, and is not much concerned with their meanings. That is why I think his error in identifying meaning and use is not of much consequence: it does not seriously affect his valuable practice. It is interesting to note, in fact, that Wittgenstein himself occasionally divorces, at least by implication, the notions of meaning and use. After describing a simple language-game involving the word 'five', he says: 'But what is the meaning of the word "five"?—No such thing was in question here, only how the word "five" is used' (P.I. §1).[3] In

[1] George Pitcher, op. cit., p. 323.

[2] This was *not* Wisdom's slogan but Wittgenstein's. Wisdom merely reported that Wittgenstein recommended this slogan at the Moral Sciences Club. See: John Wisdom, 'Ludwig Wittgenstein, 1934–37', in Fann (ed.) op. cit. p. 46.

[3] This, of course, is a rejection of the question which is one of Wittgenstein's favourite methods. See p. 64 above.

another passage, he virtually says what I have just suggested that he should have said—namely, that the philosopher ought to abandon his preoccupation with meanings and concentrate on the uses of the terms that puzzle him: [here he quotes P.I. §5].[1]

'He might better have said, . . .'; but 'this is *actually* what he does in practice'; and 'in fact, that's what he occasionally says'; while 'in another place, he *virtually* says what I have just suggested that he should have said'; etc. Instead of all these tortuous mental somersaults it would seem much easier to admit the obvious—i.e. Wittgenstein does not identify meaning with use. It seems that Pitcher is laboring under the traditional assumption that it is the job of the philosopher to give us *theories*.

There is another interesting criticism of Wittgenstein that needs to be answered. Since the goal of Wittgenstein's philosophizing is to make philosophical problems disappear, Pole wonders why don't we discover a drug which, when administered to philosophers, would cause them to lose any interest in philosophical problems?[2] It is true that Wittgenstein compared his philosophy with psycho-analysis but he explicitly attacked the suggestion that it *was* a form of psycho-analysis. 'They are different techniques', he said.[3] He also said, 'In philosophizing we may not *terminate* a disease of thought. It must run its natural course, and *slow* cure is all important' (Z. §382).[4] Philosophical problems are, of course, not psychological problems. If we speak of 'treatment' it is 'philosophical treatment'. As pointed out

[1] Pitcher, op. cit., p. 253.   [2] Pole, op. cit., p. 84.
[3] Malcolm, op. cit., p. 57.
[4] Compare: 'Why is philosophy so complicated? It ought to be *entirely* simple. Philosophy unties the knots in our thinking that we have, in a senseless way, put there. To do this it must make movements as complicated as these knots are. Although the *results* of philosophy are simple, its method cannot be, if it is to succeed. The complexity of philosophy is not its subject matter, but our knotted understanding' (P.B. §2, also Z. §452).

before, philosophical problems arise from our form of language—from the human form of life. They are 'deep' problems. That is why, in his lectures, Wittgenstein would not be satisfied until his students were thoroughly perplexed by a philosophical problem; he tried to show that 'you had confusions you never thought you could have had'.[1] He tried to work his way *into* and *through* a philosophical problem. This is reminiscent of a Zen master's procedure: 'Before you have studied Zen, mountains are mountains and rivers are rivers; while you are studying it, mountains are no longer mountains and rivers are no longer rivers; but once you have had Enlightenment, mountains are once again mountains and rivers are rivers.'[2] Something is gained by this process, i.e. *enlightenment*.

It is true that Wittgenstein says: 'The results of philosophy are the uncovering of one or another piece of plain nonsense and of bumps that the understanding has got by running its head up against the limits of language' (P.I. §119). Why, then, *encourage* people to bump their heads against the hard walls? Because 'These bumps make us see the value of discovery' (ibid.). One, so to speak, learns to *see* the limits of language (and of the world) by running his head against them. We might remember what Wittgenstein conceived himself to be doing in his 'Lecture on Ethics': 'My whole tendency and I believe the tendency of all men who ever tried to write or talk Ethics or Religion was to run against the boundaries of language.' Thus, although the successful

---

[1] D. A. T. Gasking and A. C. Jackson, 'Wittgenstein as a Teacher', in Fann (ed.), op. cit., p. 53.

[2] D. T. Suzuki, *Zen Buddhism: Selected Writings of Suzuki*, ed. by William Barrett (New York: Doubleday, 1956), pp. xvi–xvii. Wittgenstein gives a similar parable in the *Blue Book*: 'We seem to have made a discovery—which I could describe by saying that the ground on which we stood and which appeared to be firm and reliable was found to be boggy and unsafe.—That is, this happens when we philosophize; for as soon as we revert to the standpoint of common sense this *general* uncertainty disappears . . .' (B.B. p. 45).

pursuit of philosophy 'leaves everything as it is' as regards the actual use of language and our talks about mountains and rivers, it by no means leaves a philosopher as he was. He will achieve 'complete clarity' and will 'see the world aright'.

The criticisms above and many others not treated here arise from a fundamental misunderstanding of the later Wittgenstein. They are caused by reading the *Investigations* in a wrong way. The *Investigations* is completely unsystematic in both its form and its content. Unlike most earlier or later philosophical writings in the Western tradition, it consists of loosely connected remarks, unanswered questions, unamplified hints, imaginary dialogues, vague parables, metaphors, and epigrams. This, as Wittgenstein points out in the Preface, is 'connected with the very nature of the investigation'. If we ask, 'What is Wittgenstein *saying*? What kind of *theory* is he advancing?' as we usually do upon reading a philosophical book, we would be on the wrong track. I wish to suggest a way of looking at the *Investigations* which may reveal something of the 'nature' of his investigation. I recommend asking instead, 'What is Wittgenstein *doing*?' The answer is: confession and persuasion. The failure to understand what Wittgenstein was *doing* and the tendency to look for the essence of his work in a strictly rational or matter-of-fact way are the main causes of the existence of numerous wildly irrelevant interpretations and refutations of Wittgenstein.

Wittgenstein was a passionate thinker for whom philosophical problems appeared as tormenting 'personal' problems.[1] To read his philosophical diaries is to see Laocoön

---

[1] In a letter to Russell, Wittgenstein exclaimed 'I wish to God I had more understanding and everything would finally become clear to me: otherwise I cannot live any longer!' (in van Hayek, *Unfinished Sketch*). In his lectures he would exclaim with vehement sincerity: 'Philosophy is *hell*!' or 'This is as difficult as *hell*!' (See Gasking and Jackson, 'Wittgenstein as a Teacher,' op. cit., p. 52).

struggling with the serpent. Philosophy was an obsession for Wittgenstein; being a philosopher meant worrying about problems in such a concentrated way that one might at any moment go mad. Like the existentialist philosopher Wittgenstein was always in agony while doing philosophy.[1] His immediate personal aim is to rid himself of the obsession philosophical problems have become. 'The real discovery is the one that makes *me* capable of stopping doing philosophy when *I* want to' (P.I. §133, my italics). The use of first-person pronouns here is significant, it is characteristic of a confession.

The deliberately unsystematic structure of the *Investigations* is essentially related to the completely *ad hoc* character of the later work. The greater part of it, as we have seen, is devoted to criticizing the method and doctrine of the *Tractatus* and the remainder is engaged in a polemic against the prevailing tendencies of philosophizing in his time. If his criticisms sound unbearably harsh, it is because they are mainly directed against his former self. The harshness of his self-criticism calls to mind Augustine's writings. It is no wonder that he found in Augustine's *Confessions* his natural form of expression.[2]

Any serious confessions must contain, as the *Investigations* does, the full acknowledgement of temptation ('I am tempted to say here . . .', 'I felt like saying . . .', 'We are inclined to think . . .') and a willingness to correct them and give them up ('Our whole examination must be turned around . . .', 'I imposed a requirement which does not meet any real need', 'One is easily misled . . .'). As Cavell has pointed out, the voice of temptation and the voice of correction are the antagonists in Wittgenstein's dialogues.

[1] It is no accident that Wittgenstein's favourite philosophers were St. Augustine, Kierkegaard, and Dostoievsky.

[2] Stanley Cavell has called attention to this aspect of Wittgenstein's later writings in 'The Availability of Wittgenstein's Later Philosophy', *Philosophical Review* 71 (1962), p. 92.

Unlike dogmas and theories, confessions are not to be believed, criticized, or refuted. They are either honest or not honest, helpful or not helpful.

Instead of calling the *Investigations* a kind of 'confession' we may just as well call it a book of case histories of philosophic cures. He himself described it as an album of 'sketches of landscapes' made in the course of some sixteen years of 'long and involved journeyings' (Preface, p. ix). It is not case histories of different individuals but one long case history of Wittgenstein himself. The *Investigations* is, in fact, a selection and rearrangement of remarks from Wittgenstein's philosophical diaries and lecture notes taken by his students. He says in the *Investigations* 'we now demonstrate a method, by examples' (P.I. §133). He could have said: 'We now demonstrate a method of cure, by case histories.'

An important part of this method consists in providing 'reminders'. There is nothing in the *Investigations* which we should ordinarily call reasoning, argument, or proof. It is a book of *reminders*. Wittgenstein draws our attention to some very obvious facts which we forget while philosophizing. 'The work of the philosopher consists in assembling reminders for a particular purpose. If one tried to advance *theses* in philosophy, it would never be possible to debate them, because everyone would agree to them' (P.I. §127f.). This is connected to his remark in another place: 'What we are supplying are really remarks on the natural history of human beings, we are not contributing curiosities however, but observations which no one has doubted, but which have escaped remark only because they are always before our eyes' (P.I. §415; also R.F.M. p. 43). The familiar and obvious facts are most important because they are precisely the sort of things philosophers are most likely to forget (P.I. §129).

The purpose of writing a confession, recording case histories, or assembling reminders is no doubt to help others.[1] Wittgenstein's aim in philosophy is clearly stated: 'To show the fly out of the fly-bottle' (P.I. §309). He wants to help those who are obsessed by philosophical problems to achieve complete clarity, so that they are no longer tormented by those problems. Once this clarity is achieved, they can go on to do other things. Naturally Wittgenstein had a great horror of 'professorial philosophy by philosophy professors': people having to turn out lectures when they knew in their own heart that they had nothing of value to say.[2] It is with good reason that he constantly advised his students not to become professional philosophers.

Another way to characterize what he is doing is: persuasion, conversion, or even propaganda. He made this quite clear in one of his lectures: 'I am in a sense making propaganda for one style of thinking as opposed to another. I am honestly disgusted with the other. . . . Much of what I am doing is persuading the people to change their style of thinking.'[3] To this end, different methods are to be employed 'like different therapies' (P.I. §133). The sort of thing he means by 'methods' are, for example: imagining or inventing language-games as objects of comparison; calling attention to some well-known facts which are forgotten; finding and making up intermediate cases; reminding someone that the question does not arise; poking fun at a metaphysical statement to make its oddness ring; giving rules of thumb such as, 'Don't ask for meaning but ask for use'; and so on. It is worth noting here that Wittgenstein once said that a serious and good philosophical work could be written that would consist entirely of *jokes*.[4] Another time

---

[1] Not long before he died, Wittgenstein quoted to a friend the inscription that Bach wrote on his *Little Organ Book*: 'To the glory of the most high God, and that my neighbour may be benefited thereby.' Pointing to his own pile of manuscript he said: 'That is what I would have like to have been able to say about my own work.' M. Drury, 'Wittgenstein: A Symposium', in Fann (ed.), op. cit., p. 71.

[2] Ibid., p. 69.   [3] *Lectures and Conversations*, p. 28.

[4] This reminds me of the following conversation between two boys

he said that a philosophical treatise might contain nothing but questions (without answers).[1] As he put it: 'In philosophy it is always good to put a *question* instead of an answer to a question. For an answer to the philosophical question may easily be unfair; disposing of it by means of another question is not' (R.F.M. p. 68). In his own writings he made extensive use of both jokes and questions. To give a few examples: 'Why can't a dog simulate pain? Is he too honest?' (P.I. §250). 'Why can't my right hand give my left hand money?' (P.I. §268). 'Why does it sound queer to say: "For a second he felt deep grief?" Only because it so seldom happens?' (P.I. p. 174).[2] Wittgenstein employed many other devices. Which device is most suitable for a given occasion would depend on the problem and the person who is perplexed by it. He believed that no answer to a philosophical question was any good unless it came to a man when he needed it.

Wittgenstein's most important contribution to modern philosophy lies in his *method*. He is reported to have said: 'All I can give you is a method; I cannot teach you any new truths.'[3] In another lecture he remarked to the effect that it did not matter whether his results were true or not: What mattered was that 'a method had been found'.[4] His method, of course, cannot be followed as a recipe or formula, it is rather an *art*. Wittgenstein, above all, was an

[1] Malcolm, *op. cit.*, p. 29. According to Anthony Kenny, the *Investigations* contains 784 questions, only 110 of these are answered and 70 of the answers are *meant* to be wrong.

[2] This reminds me of another comic strip conversation. *Blondie*: 'What a day I had! I feel blumpy.' *Dagwood*: 'Blumpy? There is no such word in the dictionary.' *Blondie*: 'Well, that's because nobody's ever felt blumpy before.'

[3] Alice Ambrose, 'Wittgenstein on Universals', in Fann (ed.), op. cit., p. 344.

[4] Moore, op. cit., p. 322.

in a comic strip: *A*: 'Every day I ask myself those age-old philosophical questions—Who am I? Where am I? Why am I here? That, my friend, is philosophy.' *B*: 'Sounds more like amnesia.'

artist who created a new style of thinking, a new way of looking at things.

With good reasons, Wittgenstein was of the opinion that his ideas were usually misunderstood and distorted even by those who professed to be his disciples. He once told von Wright that he felt as though he were writing for people who would think in a quite different way, breathe a different air of life, from that of present-day man. For people of a different culture, as it were.[1] In the Foreword to the *Philosophische Bemerkungen* Wittgenstein writes, 'The spirit of this book is a different one from that of the mainstream of European and American civilization, in which we all stand.' It is not surprising that we should find striking resemblances between Wittgenstein's methods and that of Zen Buddhism —a philosophy from a different culture. Both Buddha and later the Zen masters were very much concerned with giving peace to those who were tormented by abstract philosophical questions. Zen masters have been particularly well known for their ability to show the nonsensicality of metaphysical questions by replying to the questioner with nonsense, a joke, an irrelevancy, a gesture, or what not. The state of 'enlightenment' in which the mind is free from philosophical questions is not unlike the state of 'complete clarity' which Wittgenstein was striving for.

Wittgenstein certainly believed that he had produced an important advance in philosophy. Yet he feared that this advance might be exaggerated. This is reflected in his choice of Nestroy's remark for the motto of the *Investigations*: 'Überhaupt hat der Fortschritt das an sich, dass er viel grösser ausschaut, als er wirklich ist.' (It is the nature of every advance, that it appears much greater than it actually is.) He was characteristically pessimistic about the future of his work. In the Preface to the *Investigations* we read: 'It is not impossible that it should fall to the lot of this work, in its

[1] G. E. von Wright, 'Biographical Sketch of Wittgenstein', in Fann (ed.), op. cit., p. 13.

poverty and in the darkness of this time, to bring light into one brain or another—but, of course, it is not likely.' I think this pessimism is connected to his profound appreciation of the 'depth' of philosophical problems.—They are deeply rooted in the human mode of life. 'The sickness of a time is cured by an alteration in the mode of life of human beings, and the sickness of philosophical problems could be cured only through a changed mode of thought and of life, not through a medicine invented by an individual' (R.F.M. p. 57).

Whether Wittgenstein's medicine is effective or not is an open question. However, judging from some of the philosophical trends arising out of his work, Wittgenstein's fear—'The seed I am most likely to sow is a certain jargon' —was not totally unfounded.[1]

[1] *Wittgenstein's Lectures in the Spring of 1939*, the concluding remark of this series of lectures.

Bibliography*

I. WORKS BY WITTGENSTEIN (1889–1951)

(In Order of Composition)

'Notes on Logic' (Sept, 1913). Edited by H. T. Costello, *The Journal of Philosophy* 54 (1957), 230–44. Reprinted in *Notebooks 1914–16*. See Anscombe, etc. and Kurtz in II. C.

'Notes Dictated to Moore in Norway' (April 1914). Reprinted in *Notebooks 1914–16*, 107–18.

Notebooks 1914–16. Edited by G. E. M. Anscombe and G. H. von Wright with an English translation by G. E. M. Anscombe. Oxford: Basil Blackwell, 1961; New York: Barnes & Noble, 1961; New York: Harper & Row, 1968, paper.

Letters to Russell, 1912–21. Some extracts contained in *Notebooks 1914–16*.

Logisch-philosophische Abhandlung (finished in 1918). First published in *Annalen der Naturphilosophie* 14 (1921), 185–262.

Tractatus Logico-Philosophicus, with an introduction by Bertrand Russell. English edition of *Logisch-philosophische Abhandlung* with an English translation by C. K. Ogden. London: Routledge & Kegan Paul, 1922; 2nd impression with a few corrections, 1933.

[*I would like to thank my many friends who have contributed to this bibliography. Special thanks are due to the staff of the Cleveland State University Library who have been most helpful in obtaining copies of many of the articles in this bibliography for me. Any corrections and additions will be most welcome.]

A new English translation by D. F. Pears and B. F. McGuinness. London: Routledge & Kegan Paul, 1961.

Italian edition: Translation, introduction, and notes by G. C. M. Colombo (Milano-Roma: Fratelli Bocca, 1954). A new Italian translation with *Notebooks* by Amendo G. Conte (Torino, 1964).

Russian edition: Translated by I. Dobronravov and D. Laxuti with an introduction by V. Asmus and commentary by D. Laxuti, V. Finn, D. Kuznecov and I. Dobronravov (Moscow, 1958).

French edition (together with the *Philosophical Investigations*): Translated by Pierre Klossowski (Paris: Gallimard, 1961).

Swedish edition: Translation, introduction, and notes by A. Wedberg (Stockholm: Orion/Bonniers, 1962).

Danish edition: Translation, introduction, and notes by D. Favrholdt (Copenhagen: Gyldendal, 1963).

Chinese edition (*Ming Li Lun*): Translated by Chang Shen-Fu, appeared in *Che-Hsüeh Ping-Lun* (Peking), Vol. 1, No. 5 (1927), 53–98, and Vol. 1, No. 6 (1928), 31–80.

Hungarian edition: Translated by Gyorgy Márkus (Budapest: Akadémiai Kiadó, 1963).

Spanish edition: Translated by T. Galván (Madrid: Revista de Occidente, 1957).

Yugoslavian edition: Translated by G. Petrović (Sarajevo: Veselin Maslesa, 1960).

Wörterbuch für Volksschulen. Wien: Hölder-Pichler-Tempsky, 1926. A spelling book for elementary schools, containing between 6000 and 7000 words.

'Some Remarks on Logical Form', *Proceedings of the Aristotelian Society*, Suppl. Vol. 9 (1929), 162–71. Reprinted with a note by Anscombe in Copi and Beard (eds.), *Essays on Tractatus*.

'A Lecture on Ethics' (1930). *The Philosophical Review* 74 (1965), 3–12.

Philosophische Bemerkungen (1930). Edited by Rush Rhees. Oxford: Basil Blackwell, 1965; Frankfurt: Suhrkamp.

Philosophische Grammatik (1932). A 768 page typescript 'divided into titled chapters and sections, as in conventional learned works'. Edited by Rush Rhees. Oxford: Basil Blackwell; Frankfurt: Suhrkamp, 1969.

'Bemerkungen Über Frazers *The Golden Bough*' (one set in 1931, the other much later). Edited with a note by Rush Rhees. *Synthese* 17 (1967), 233–53.

Letter to The Editor. *Mind* 42 (1933), 415–16.

The Blue and Brown Books (1933–35). Edited with a preface by Rush Rhees (Oxford: Basil Blackwell, 1st edition 1958, 2nd edition (with an index) 1969. French translation with introduction by Jean Wahl (Paris: Gallimard, 1965). Hardback edition (New York: Barnes & Noble, 1968). Paperback edition (New York: Harper & Row, 1965).

'Notes for Lectures on "Private Experience" and "Sense Data" ' (1935–36). Edited with a note by Rush Rhees, published in the *Philosophical Review* 77 (1968), 271–320.

Remarks on the Foundations of Mathematics (1937–44). German text edited by G. H. von Wright, R. Rhees, and G. E. M. Anscombe with an English translation by G. E. M. Anscombe. Oxford: Basil Blackwell, 1st editon 1956, 2nd edition 1967. Hardback edition, New York: Barnes & Noble, 1962. Paper edition, Cambridge, Mass.: M.I.T. Press, 1967. A long excerpt (60 pages) is included in P. Benacerraf and H. Putnam (eds.), *Philosophy of Mathematics* (Prentice-Hall, 1964). A selection in German appeared in *Kursbuch* 8 (1967), 93–105. Another selection entitled 'Remarks on Mechanical Mathematics' is included in K. M. Sayre and F. J. Crosson (eds.), *The Modelling of Mind: Computers and Intelligence* (Simon & Schuster, 1968), 121–40.

Lectures and Conversations on Aesthetics, Psychology and Religious Belief (1938). Compiled from notes taken by Y. Smythies, R. Rhees and J. Taylor; edited by Cyril Barrett. Oxford: Basil Blackwell; Berkeley: University of California Press, 1966.

Philosophical Investigations (Part I finished in 1945; Part II written between 1947 and 1949). English edition of *Philosophische Untersuchungen*, edited by G. E. M. Anscombe and R. Rhees with an English translation by G. E. M. Anscombe. Oxford: Basil Blackwell, 1st edition 1953, 2nd edition 1958, 3rd edition (with an index) 1967. New York: Macmillan, 1953. French translation by P. Klossowski, Paris, 1961.

Zettel (1945–48). Edited by G. E. M. Anscombe and G. H. von Wright with an English translation by G. E. M. Anscombe. Oxford: Basil Blackwell, 1967; Berkeley: University of California Press, 1967.

On Certainty (1950–51). Edited by G. E. M. Anscombe and G. H. von Wright, with an English translation by D. Paul and G. E. M. Anscombe. Oxford: Basil Blackwell; New York: Harper & Row, 1969.

Schriften. Includes: *Tractatus Logico-Philosophicus*, *Tagebücher 1914–16*, *Philosophische Untersuchungen* etc. Frankfurt: Suhrkamp Verlag, 1960–.

WAISMANN, F. 'Abschrift von Reden und Gesprächen zwischen Dezember 1929 und September 1931.' Selections from his shorthand notes to Wittgenstein's talks and discussions with him and Schlick from 1929 to 1931. Included in *Philosophische Bemerkungen*, 317–46.

—. 'Notes on Talks with Wittgenstein.' Two selections on Ethics: Dec. 30th, 1929, and Dec. 17th, 1930. Published with an English translation by Max Black in *The Philosophical Review* 74 (1965), 12–16.

—. *Wittgenstein und der Wiener Kreis* (Conversations recorded by Waismann). Edited with an Introduction by B. F. McGuinness. Oxford: Basil Blackwell; German edition only, 1967. (Waismann's notes of Wittgenstein's conversations with him and Schlick during 1929–31.) Includes Waismann's *Thesen*, an attempt to codify Wittgenstein's early philosophy, which circulated among members of the Vienna Circle in 1930.

ENGELMANN, PAUL. *Letters from Wittgenstein with a Memoir*. Translated by L. Furtmüller, edited with an appendix by B. F. McGuinness. Oxford: Basil Blackwell, 1967. (There are about 50 letters from 1916 to 1937; also included is a short account of Engelmann by Dr. Josef Schächter.) New York: Horizon Press, 1968.

ECCLES, W. 'Some Letters of Wittgenstein, 1912–1939.' *Hermathena* (Dublin), No. 97 (1963), 57–65.

MOORE, G. E. 'Wittgenstein's Lectures in 1930–33.' Part I, *Mind* 63 (1954), 1–15; Part II, *Mind* 63 (1954), 289–315; Part III, *Mind* 64 (1955), 1–27; 'Two Corrections', *Mind* 64 (1955), 264. Reprinted in his *Philosophical Papers* and in R. Ammerman (ed.): *Classics in Analytic Philosophy* (New York: McGraw-Hill, 1965).

AMBROSE, ALICE AND MARGARET MASTERMAN. *The Yellow Book* (1933–34). Notes taken by Ambrose and Masterman in the intervals between dictation of *The Blue Book*. See Bouwsma's 'The Blue Book'. Some quotations from it appeared in Alice Ambrose and Morris Lazerowitz's writings on Wittgenstein.

MACDONALD, MARGARET. *Notes of Wittgenstein's Lectures in 1934–35*. Unpublished. A typed copy of Lectures 8–15 (May 20th, 1935–June 12th, 1935) is appended to a typewritten copy of the *Blue Book* on deposit at the University of Southern California Library.

MALCOLM, NORMAN. *Wittgenstein's Lectures on the Foundations of Mathematics*. Notes by Malcolm of Wittgenstein's lectures given in the spring of 1939. In private circulation.

GEACH, PETER. *Wittgenstein's Lectures on Philosophical Psychology*. Notes taken by Geach of Wittgenstein's lectures in 1946–47. There exist two other sets of notes from the same course of lectures; one by K. Shah, the other by A. G. Jackson. In private circulation.

II. WRITINGS ON WITTGENSTEIN

A. Books

AMBROSE, ALICE. *Essays in Analysis*. London: George Allen & Unwin; New York: Humanities Press, 1966.

ANSCOMBE, G. E. M. *An Introduction to Wittgenstein's Tractatus*. London: Hutchinson, 1959; 2nd edition, revised: Harper Torch book, 1963.

BARONE, FRANCESCO. *Il Neopositivismo Logico*. Torino: Edizioni di Filosofia, 1951.

BLACK, MAX. *A Companion to Wittgenstein's Tractatus*. Ithaca, N.Y.: Cornell University Press, 1964. Translated into Italian by R. Simone. Rome: Ubaldini Editore, 1967.

CAMPANALE, D. *Studi su Wittgenstein*. Bari: Adriatica Editrice, 1956.

— *Problemi Epistemologici de Hume all' Ultimo Wittgenstein*. Bari: Adriatica Editrice, 1961.

CHARLESWORTH, MAXWELL J. *Philosophy and Linguistic Analysis*. Pittsburgh: Duquesne University Press, 1959.

COPI, I. M., AND R. W. BEARD (eds.). *Essays on Wittgenstein's Tractatus*. New York: Macmillan; London: Routledge & Kegan Paul, 1966.

CORNFORTH, MAURICE. *Marxism and Linguistic Philosophy*. London: Lawrence & Wishart, 1965; New York: International Publishers, 1965.

DE MAURO, TULLIO. *Ludwig Wittgenstein: His Place in and Influence on the History of Semantics*. (Foundations of Language Supplementary Series, Vol. 3.) Dordrecht, Holland: D. Reidel Publishing Co., 1967.

FANN, K. T. (ed.). *Wittgenstein, The Man and His Philosophy. An Anthology*. A Delta book. New York: Dell, 1967.

FAVRHOLDT, DAVID. *An Interpretation and Critique of Wittgenstein's Tractatus*. Copenhagen, Denmark: Munksgaard, 1964. New York: Humanities Press, 1966.

FEIBLEMAN, JAMES. *Inside the Great Mirror* (Examination of the Philosophy of Russell, Wittgenstein, and their Followers). The Hague: Martinus Nijhoff, 1958.

GALLIE, W. B. *The Distinction Between Theory and Practice, From Plato to Wittgenstein.* Forthcoming from the Bobbs-Merrill Co., Inc., Indianapolis.

GANGULY, SACHINDRANATH. *Logical Positivism as a Theory of Meaning.* Calcutta: Allied Publishers, 1967.

GARGANI, ALDO G. *Linguaggio ed Esperienza in Ludwig Wittgenstein.* Firenze: Felice Le Monnier, 1966.

GELLNER, ERNEST. *Words and Things*: A Critical Account of Linguistic Philosophy and a Study in Ideology. Boston: Beacon Press, 1960; the Pelican edition, 1968.

GRIFFIN, J. *Wittgenstein's Logical Atomism.* London: Oxford University Press, 1964.

HALLETT, GARTH. *Wittgenstein's Definition of Meaning as Use.* Bronx: Fordham University Press, 1967.

HARTNACK, JUSTUS. *Wittgenstein and Modern Philosophy.* Translated by Maurice Cranston. (Originally published in Danish, 1960; German translation, Stuttgart, 1962). New York: Anchor Books, Doubleday, 1965.

VAN HAYEK, F. A. *Unfinished Draft of a Sketch of a Biography of Wittgenstein* (written in 1953 for private circulation). A very interesting and informative account of Wittgenstein's life up to 1929, unpublished.

HENZE, DONALD F. and JOHN T. SAUNDERS. *The Private-Language Problem: A Philosophical Dialogue.* New York: Random House, 1967.

HESTER, MARCUS B. *The Meaning of Poetic Metaphor: An Analysis in the Light of Wittgenstein's Claim that Meaning is Use.* The Hague: Mouton & Co., 1967.

HIGH, DALLAS M. *Language, Persons, and Belief.* (Studies in Wittgenstein's *Philosophical Investigations* and Religious Use of Language.) New York: Oxford University Press, 1967.

HUDSON, DONALD. *Ludwig Wittgenstein: The Bearing of his Philosophy upon Religious Belief.* London: Lutterworth Press; Richmond, Virginia: John Knox Press, 1968.

KIELKOPF, CHARLES. *Strict Finitism: An Examination of Wittgenstein's Remarks on Mathematics.* The Hague: Mouton & Co., 1970.

MALCOLM, NORMAN. *Ludwig Wittgenstein: A Memoir.* (With a Biographical Sketch by von Wright and a photograph.) London: Oxford University Press, 1958. Revised edition, 1966. German edition: R. Oldenbourg Verlag, Munchen und Wien.

MASLOW, ALEXANDER. *A Study in Wittgenstein's Tractatus.* Berkeley: University of California Press, 1961.

MORICK, HAROLD (ed.): *Wittgenstein and the Problem of Other Minds.* New York: McGraw-Hill, 1967.

MORRISON, JAMES C. *Meaning and Truth in Wittgenstein's Tractatus.* The Hague: Mouton & Co., 1968.

MULLIN, A. A. *Philosophical Comments on the Philosophies of C. S. Peirce and Ludwig Wittgenstein.* Urbana, Illinois: Electrical Engineering Research Laboratory, Engineering Experiment Station, University of Illinois, 1961.

MÜLLER, A. *Ontologie in Wittgenstein's "Tractatus".* Bonn: H. Bouvier u. Co. Verlag, 1967.

NAESS, ARNE. *Moderne Filosoffer: Carnap, Wittgenstein, Heidegger, Sartre.* Copenhagen: Stjernebogerne Vintens Forlag, 1965. English translation by Alastair Hannay, 1968.

PINSENT, DAVID. *Excerpts on Wittgenstein from the Diary of David Pinsent, 1912–14,* on deposit at Trinity College, Cambridge University.

PITCHER, GEORGE. *The Philosophy of Wittgenstein.* Englewood Cliffs, N.J.: Prentice-Hall, 1964.

PITCHER, GEORGE (ed.). *Wittgenstein: The Philosophical Investigations* (A Collection of Critical Essays). An Anchor Book. New York: Doubleday, 1966.

PLOCHMANN, G. K. and J. B. LAWSON. *Terms in their Propositional Contexts in Wittgenstein's Tractatus: An Index.* Carbondale: Southern Illinois University Press, 1962.

POLE, DAVID. *The Later Philosophy of Wittgenstein*. London: The Athlone Press, University of London, 1958.

RAO, A. PAMPAPATHY. *A Survey of Wittgenstein's Theory of Meaning*. Calcutta: Indian University Press, 1965.

RIVERSO, EMANUELE. *Il Pensiero di Ludovico Wittgenstein*. Napoli: Liberia Scientifica Editrice, 1964.

—. *L. Wittgenstein e il Simbolisimo Logico*. Napoli, 1956.

ROLLINS, C. D. (ed.). *Knowledge and Experience*. Pittsburgh: University of Pittsburgh Press, 1962. Includes two symposia on Wittgenstein, see Castañeda and Garver in II.C.

SCHULZ, WALTER. *Wittgenstein: Die Negation der Philosophie*. Stuttgart: Verlag Günther Neske Pfullingen, 1967.

SPECHT, ERNEST KONRAD. *Die sprachphilosophischen und ontologischen Grundlagen im Spätwerk Ludwig Wittgensteins*. *Kantstudien*, Ergänzungsheft 84, Köln: Kölner Universitätsverlag, 1963. English translation: *The Foundations of Wittgenstein's Late Philosophy*, by D. E. Walford. Manchester University Press, 1967.

STENIUS, E. *Wittgenstein's Tractatus*. Oxford: Basil Blackwell, 1960.

WAISMANN, F. *The Principles of Linguistic Philosophy*. Edited by R. Harré. London: Macmillan & Co.; New York: St. Martin's Press, 1968.

WEINBERG, J. R. *An Examination of Logical Positivism*. London: Routledge & Kegan Paul, Ltd., 1936. Paperback edition, New Jersey: Littlefield, Adams & Co., 1960.

Über Ludwig Wittgenstein. With contributions by Norman Malcolm, Peter Strawson, Newton Garver and Stanley Cavell. Frankfurt: Suhrkamp Verlag, 1968.

Wittgenstein Schriften/Beiheft: Arbeiten über Wittgenstein. Mit Beitragen von I. Bachmann, M. Cranston, J. Ferrata Mora, P. Feyerabend, E. Heller, B. Russell, and G. H. von Wright. Frankfurt: Suhrkamp Verlag, 1960.

B. Dissertations

ALLAIRE, EDWIN B., JR. *A Critical Examination of Wittgenstein's 'Tractatus'*. Ph.D. dissertation. State University of Iowa, 1960.

AMDUR, STEPHEN. *Toward An Understanding of the Later Philosophy of Wittgenstein*. M.A. Thesis. University of New Mexico, 1967.

BERLINSKI, DAVID. *The Well-Tempered Wittgenstein: A Study of the Picture Theory of Meaning*. Ph.D. dissertation. Princeton University, 1967.

BUCHANAN, RUPERT. *Wittgenstein's Discussion of Sensation*. Ph.D. dissertation. Duke University, 1966.

BURLINGAME, CHARLES E. *On the Logic of 'Seeing As' Locution*. Ph.D. dissertation. University of Virginia, 1965.

CAVELL, STANLEY. *The Claim to Rationality*. Ph.D. dissertation. Harvard University, 1961.

CROWE, CHARLES L. A *New Estimate of the Significance of Wittgenstein's 'Tractatus' for the Analysis of Theological Discourse*. Ph.D. dissertation. Columbia University, 1961.

GARVER, NEWTON. *Grammar and Criteria*. Ph.D. dissertation. Cornell University, 1965.

GIBBS, B. R. *Wittgenstein and the Problem of Meaning*. M.A. Thesis. University of Canterbury (New Zealand), 1961.

GINNANE, W. J. *Thought, Language and Behavior*. With particular reference to the later works of Wittgenstein. M.A. Thesis. University of Melbourne (Australia), 1958.

GRANT, BRIAN. *Wittgenstein on Pain and Privacy*. Ph.D. dissertation. University of California (Irvine), 1968.

GRIFFITH, WILLIAM B. *Problems About Infinity: Wittgenstein's Contribution*. Ph.D. dissertation. Yale University, 1963.

GUSTASON, WILLIAM. *Negation and Assertion in Frege and the Tractatus*. Ph.D. dissertation. University of Michigan, 1968.

HARDWICK, CHARLES S. *Wittgenstein's Later Philosophy of Language*. Ph.D. dissertation. University of Texas, 1967.

HARRIS, C. EDWARD. *Wittgenstein's Criticism of Ostensive Explanation*. Ph.D. dissertation. Vanderbilt University, 1966.

HICKS, J. R. *Language-Games and Inner Experience*. Ph.D. dissertation. University College (London), 1961.

KIRKBY, RONALD V. *The Other Mind Quandary*. Ph.D. dissertation. University of California, Berkeley, 1966.

LANFEAR, J. RAY. *An analysis of Wittgenstein's Locution 'Meaning As Use'*. Ph.D. dissertation. Rice University, 1968.

LEWIS, HARRY A. *Criteria, Theory and Knowledge of Other Minds*. Ph.D. dissertation. Stanford University, 1967.

LONG, THOMAS A. *Wittgenstein, Criteria, and Private Experience*. Ph.D. dissertation. University of Cincinnati, 1965.

MORAN, JOHN HENRY. *Ludwig Wittgenstein's Philosophical Therapy*. Ph.D. dissertation. Fordham University, 1962.

MORICK, HAROLD. *Wittgenstein's Attack on the Privileged Access View of Thoughts and Feelings*. Ph.D. dissertation. Columbia University, 1966.

O'BRIEN, GEORGE D. *Meaning and Fact: A Study in the Philosophy of Wittgenstein*. Ph.D. dissertation. University of Chicago, 1961.

RUDDICK, SARA L. *Wittgenstein on Sensation Statements*. Ph.D. dissertation. Harvard University, 1963.

SANDERSON, DONALD G. *The Philosophical Methods of Wittgenstein's Philosophical Investigations*. M.A. Thesis. Florida State University, 1969.

SHAW, J. W. *The Influence of the Later Philosophy of Wittgenstein upon the Philosophy of Mind*. M.A. Thesis. Bangor College (Wales), 1962.

SHWAYDER, D. S. *Wittgenstein's Tractatus: A Historical and Critical Commentary*. Ph.D. dissertation. Oxford University, 1954.

SIEVERT, DONALD. *Wittgenstein, Strawson, and Austin on the Problem of Other Minds*. Ph.D. dissertation. University of Iowa, 1968.

SIVASAMBU, N. *Some Problems in the 'Tractatus'*. M.A. Thesis. University College (London), 1961.

SMERUD, WARREN D. *Can There Be a Private Language? A Review of Some Principal Arguments*. Ph.D. dissertation. University of Washington, 1967.

TOLAND, WILLIAM G. *The Later Wittgenstein and Classical Pragmatism: A Critical Appraisal.* Ph.D. dissertation. University of North Carolina, 1967.

WIEBENGA, W. *Wittgenstein's Theory of Meaning.* Ph.D. dissertation. Yale University, 1966.

ZWEIG, ARNULF. *Theories of Real Definition: A Study of the Views of Aristotle, C. I. Lewis, and Wittgenstein.* Ph.D. dissertation. Stanford University, 1960.

C. Articles and Chapters

AARON, R. I. 'Wittgenstein's Theory of Universals.' *Mind* 74 (1965), 249–51.

ABBAGNANO N. 'L'ultimo Wittgenstein.' *Revista de Filosofia* 44 (1953), 447–56.

AGASSI, JOSEPH. Letter. *Times* (London) *Literary Supplement* (May 22nd, 1959), 9. A reply to the letter is included.

—. Letter. *Ibid.* (May 29th, 1959), 321.

A.G.C. (signed by). 'Notice of the New English translation of *Tractatus*.' *Revista di Filosofia* 53 (1962), 92.

—. 'Notice of *Schriften, Beiheft* and *Hartnack*.' *Ibid.*, 356–8.

—. 'Notice of the French ed. of *Tractatus* and *Investigations*.' *Ibid.*, 222.

ALBRITTON, R. 'On Wittgenstein's Use of the Term "Criterion".' *Journal of Philosophy* 56 (1959), 845–57; reprinted in Pitcher.

—. 'Knowledge and Doubt.' Isenberg lecture delivered on Nov. 8, 1968 at the Michigan State University.

ALDRICH, V. C. 'Images as Things and Things as Imaged.' *Mind* 64 (1955), 261–3.

—. 'Pictorial Meaning, Picture-Thinking, and Wittgenstein's Theory of Aspects.' *Mind* 67 (1958), 70–9.

—. 'Image-Mongering and Image-Management.' *Philosophy and Phenomenological Research* 23 (1962), 51–61.

ALDWINCLE, R. F. 'Much Ado about Words; Some Reflections on Language, Philosophy, and Theology (review article).' *Canadian Journal of Theology* 7 (1961), 91–8.

ALLAIRE, EDWIN B. 'Tractatus 6.3751.' Analysis 19 (1959), 100–5; reprinted in Copi and Beard.

—. 'The Tractatus: Nominalistic or Realistic', in E. B. Allaire and Others (ed.): Essays in Ontology (The Hague: Martinus Nijhoff, 1963), 148–65; reprinted in Copi and Beard.

—. 'Types and Formation Rules: A Note on Tractatus 3.334.' Analysis 21 (1961). 14–6.

—. 'Things, Relations and Identity.' Philosophy of Science 34 (1967), 260–72.

A.M. (signed by). 'Notice of Gargani and High.' Review of Metaphysics 22 (1968), 144–5.

ALSTON, WILLIAM P. 'Introduction to Part IX: Ordinary Language Philosophy', in Alston and George Nakhnikian (eds.): Readings in 20th-Century Philosophy (New York: The Free Press, 1963), 495–512.

AMBROSE, ALICE. 'Finitism in Mathematics.' Mind 44 (1935), 186–203; 317–40.

—. 'Are There Three Consecutive Sevens in the Expansion of π?' Michigan Academy of Science, Arts and Letters, 1936.

—. 'Finitism and the Limits of Empiricism.' Mind 46 (1937), 379–85, a revised version reprinted in her Essays in Analysis.

—. 'Proof and Theorem Proved.' (Abstract). Journal of Philosophy 55 (1958), 901–2. See comments by Swanson.

—. 'Proof and the Theorem Proved.' Mind 68 (1959), 435–45; reprinted in her Essays in Analysis. See Castañeda.

—. 'Review of Investigations.' Philosophy and Phenomenological Research 15 (1954), 111–5.

—. 'Wittgenstein on Some Questions in Foundations of Mathematics.' Journal of Philosophy 52 (1955), 197–213. Reprinted in her Essays in Analysis, and in Fann.

—. 'Review of Remarks on the Foundations of Mathematics.' Phil. and Phen. Research 18 (1957), 262–5.

—. 'Review of Pitcher.' Ibid. 25 (1965), 423–5.

—. 'Wittgenstein on Universals', in W. E. Kennick and M. Lazerowitz (eds.): *Metaphysics: Readings and Reappraisals* (Englewood Cliffs, N.J.: Prentice-Hall, 1966), 80–91. Reprinted in her *Essays in Analysis* and in Fann.

—. 'Metamorphoses of the Principle of Verifiability', in F. C. Dommeyer (ed.): *Current Philosophical Issues, Essays in Honor of C. J. Ducasse* (Springfield, Ill.: Charles C. Thomas, 1966).

—. 'Invention and Discovery', in her *Essays in Analysis*, 66–87.

—. 'Internal Relations.' *Review of Metaphysics* 21 (1968), 256–61.

AMBROSE, ALICE and M. LAZEROWITZ. 'Wittgenstein: Philosophy, Experiment and Proof', in C. A. Mace (ed.): *British Philosophy in the Mid-Century* (London: George Allen & Unwin, 1966 revised edition). Part I reprinted in Fann.

AMMERMAN, R. R. 'Wittgenstein's Later Methods' (Abstract). *Journal of Philosophy* 58 (1961), 707–8.

ANDERSON, A. R. 'Mathematics and the "Language Game".' *Review of Metaphysics* 11 (1958), 446–58. Reprinted in P. Benacerraf and H. Putnam (eds.): *Philosophy of Mathematics* (Englewood Cliffs, N.J.: Prentice-Hall, 1965).

ANDERSON, PERRY. 'Components of the National Culture.' *New Left Review* No. 50 (1968), 21–5 on Wittgenstein.

ANSCOMBE, G. E. M. 'Mr Copi on Objects, Properties and Relations in the *Tractatus*.' *Mind* 68 (1959), 404; reprinted in Copi and Beard.

—. 'Note on the English Version of Wittgenstein's *Philosophische Untersuchungen*.' *Mind* 62 (1953), 521–2.

—. 'What Wittgenstein Really Said.' *Tablet* (April 17th, 1954), 373.

—. Letter. *Tablet* (May 15th, 1954), 478–9. A reply to Colombo.

—. Letter. *Times Lit. Suppl.* (May 29th, 1959), 321.

—. 'Wittgenstein.' *World Review* (Jan. 1952), 3. Corrections of Cranston (1951).

—. 'Retraction.' *Analysis* 26 (1965), 33–6. See Stenius.

ANSCOMBE, G. E. M., R. RHEES, and G. H. VON WRIGHT. 'A Note on Costello's Version of the "Notes on Logic".' *Journal of Philosophy* 54 (1957), 484. See Kurtz.

—. 'Letter from Wittgenstein's Literary Executors.' *Mind* 60 (1951), 584.

ANTONELLI, MA. TERESA. 'A proposito del ultimo Wittgenstein: Observaciones sobre el convencionalismo.' *Crisis* (Madrid) 3, No. 12 (Octubre–diciembre, 1956), 473–84.

APEL, KARL-OTTO. 'Wittgenstein und das Problem des Hermeneutischen Verstehens.' *Zeitschrift für Theologie und Kirche* 63 (1966), 49–87.

—. 'Die Entfaltung der »sprachanalytischen« Philosophie und das Problem der »Geisteswissenschaften«.' *Philosophisches Jahrbuch* 72 (1965), 239–89.

APOSTEL, L. 'Review of *Tractatus*.' *Revue Internationale de Philosophie* 9 (1955), 439.

ARBINI, R. 'Frederick Ferré on Colour Incompatibility.' *Mind* 72 (1963), 586–90.

ARRINGTON, ROBERT L. 'Wittgenstein on Contradiction.' *Southern Journal of Philosophy* 7 (1969), 37–44.

AUNE, BRUCE. 'Knowing and Merely Thinking.' *Philosophical Studies* 12, No. 4 (1960), 53–8. (See King-Farlow).

—. 'On the Complexity of Avowals', in M. Black (ed.), *Philosophy in America* (Cornell University Press, 1965), 35–57.

—. 'Does Knowledge Have an Indubitable Foundation?' etc. in his *Knowledge, Mind, and Nature* (New York: Random House, 1967), 31–62.

AYER, A. J. 'Atomic Propositions.' *Analysis* 1, No. 1 (1933), 2–6.

—. 'Can There Be a Private Language?' *Proceedings of the Aristotelian Society*, Supplementary Volume 28 (1954), 63–76; reprinted in Ayer's *The Concept of A Person* (New York: St. Martin's, 1963), in Pitcher, and in Morick.

—. 'Wittgenstein.' Review of *Blue and Brown Books* and Malcolm's *Memoir. Spectator* 201 (Nov. 14th, 1958), 654.

BACHMANN, INGEBORG. 'Zu einem Kapitel der jüngsten Philosophiegeschichte', in *Wittgenstein Schriften/Beiheft,* 7–15.

BAIER, KURT. 'Ludwig Wittgenstein.' *Meanjin* (Australia) (March, 1960), 84–7.

BAMBROUGH, J. R. 'Universals and Family Resemblances.' *Proceedings of the Aristotelian Society* 61 (1960–61), 207–22; reprinted in Pitcher.

—. 'Principia Metaphysica.' *Philosophy* 39 (1964), 97–109.

BARONE, FRANCESCO. 'El Solipsismo Linguistico di Ludwig Wittgenstein.' *Filosofia* 2 (1951), 543–70.

—. 'L. Wittgenstein', in *Enciclopedia Filosofica,* Vol. IV (Venezia: Instituto per la Colloborazione Culturale), 1957.

—. 'Wittgenstein: *Philosophical Investigations.*' *Filosofia* 4 (1953), 680–91.

—. 'Review of *Investigations.*' *Giornale Critico della Filosofia Italiana* 33 (1954), 109–17.

—. 'Wittgenstein Inedito.' *Filosofia della Scienza* 4 (Torino, 1953), 5–16.

BARRETT, C. 'Les Leçons de Wittgenstein sur l'esthétique.' *Archives de Philosophie* 28 (1965), 5–22.

BARRETT, C., MARGARET PATON, and HARRY BLOCKER. 'Wittgenstein and Problems of Objectivity in Aesthetics.' A Symposium. *British Journal of Aesthetics* 7 (1967), 158–74.

BEARD, R. W. '*Tractatus* 4.24.' *Southern Journal of Philosophy* 2 (1964), 14–17.

BEGIASVILI, A. F. 'Analysis and Mysticism', in his *The Analytic Method in Contemporary Bourgeois Philosophy* (Tbilisi, Idz. An Gruzinskoj SSR, 1960), 56–71

BEHL, L. 'Wittgenstein and Heidegger.' *Duns Scotus Philosophical Association Convention Report* 27 (1963), 70–115.

BEJERHOLM, L. 'Logikn i "Guds Ledning".' *Svensk Teologisk Kvartalskift* 41 (1965), 25–38.

BELL, JULIAN. 'An Epistle on the Subject of the Ethical and Aesthetic Beliefs of Herr Ludwig Wittgenstein', in Sherard Vines (ed.): *Whips and Scorpions: Specimens of Modern Satiric Verse, 1914–31* (London: Wishart, 1932), 21–30; reprinted in Copi and Beard.

BELL, RICHARD H. 'Names and the Picture Theory in Use.' *Graduate Review of Philosophy* (University of Minnesota), 4 (1962), 20–8.

BENACERRAF, PAUL and HILARY PUTNAM. 'Wittgenstein', A section in their introduction to *Philosophy of Mathematics* (selected readings), 25–38.

BENNETT, JONATHAN. 'Reviews of Copi's Article in *Mind* (1958), Anscombe's Comments in *Mind* (1959), Evans' in *Mind* (1959), and Copi's in *Analysis* (1958).' *Journal of Symbolic Logic* 27, No. 1 (1962), 118–20.

—. 'On Being Forced to a Conclusion.' *Proceedings of the Aristotelian Society*, Suppl. Vol. 35 (1961), 15–34. See Wood.

—. 'Review of Pitcher.' *Philosophy* 41 (1966), 86–7.

BERGGREN, DOUGLAS. 'Language Games and Symbolic Forms' (abstract). *Journal of Philosophy* 58 (1961), 708–9.

BERGMANN, GUSTAV. 'The Glory and the Misery of Ludwig Wittgenstein', in his *Logic and Reality* (Wisconsin University Press, 1964), 225–41; reprinted in Copi and Beard. Italian translation by A. G. Conte appeared in *Rivista di Filosofia* 52 (1961), 387–406.

—. 'Stenius on Wittgenstein's *Tractatus*.' *Theoria* 29, Part 2 (1963), 176–204; reprinted in his *Logic and Reality*. op. cit., 174–82.

BERLIN, ISAIAH. 'Review of Weinberg.' *Criterion* 17 (1937), 174–82.

BERNAYS, PAUL. 'Comments on L. Wittgenstein's *Remarks on the Foundations of Mathematics*.' *Ratio* 2 (1959), 1–22. Reprinted with an English translation in Benacerraf and Putnam (eds.): *Philosophy of Mathematics*.

BERNSTEIN, R. J. 'Notice of *Notebooks*.' *Review of Metaphysics* 15 (1961), 197.

—. 'Notice of *Tractatus*.' *Ibid.* 15 (1962), 681.

—. 'Notice of Pitcher (ed.)'. *Ibid.* 20 (1967), 557.

—. 'Notice of *Zettel*.' *Ibid.* 22 (1968), 158.

—. 'Wittgenstein's Three Languages.' *Ibid.* 15 (1961), 278–98; reprinted in Copi and Beard.

BERRY, G. D. W. 'Review of *Remarks*.' *Philosophical Forum* 16 (1958–59), 73–5.

BHARATI, A. 'Review of Pole.' *Zeitschrift für Philosophische Forschung* 16 (1962), 158–60.

BLACK, MAX. 'Critical Notice of *Notebooks*.' *Mind* 73 (1964), 132–41.

—. 'Relation Between Logical Positivism and the Cambridge School of Analysis.' *Erkenntnis* 8 (1939–40), 24–35.

—. 'Review of Plochmann and Lawson.' *Philosophical Review* 72 (1963), 265–6.

—. 'Review of Griffin.' *Philosophical Quarterly* 16 (1966), 374–6.

—. 'Some Problems Connected with Language.' *Proceedings of the Aristotelian Society* 39 (1938–39), 43–68; reprinted as 'Wittgenstein's *Tractatus*' in his *Language and Philosophy* (Cornell University Press, 1944), and in Copi and Beard.

—. 'Wittgenstein: An (unauthorized) report of some of his views on pure mathematics, which constitute, by implication and explicitly, a thorough repudiation of the logistic thesis', in his *The Nature of Mathematics* (London, 1933), 129–34.

BLANCHÉ, R. 'Review of Griffin.' *Revue Philosophique* (1967, No. 3), 420–1.

BLANSHARD, BRAND. 'Logical Atomism' and 'Linguistic Philosophy', in his *Reason and Analysis* (La Salle, Illinois: Open Court, 1962).

BLUMBERG, A. E. and H. FEIGL. 'Logical Positivism: A New Movement in European Philosophy.' *Journal of Philosophy* 28 (1931), 281–96.

BOBBIO, N. 'Review of Malcolm's *Memoir*.' *Rivista de Filosofia* 50 (1959), 233–4.

BOGEN, JAMES. 'Was Wittgenstein a Psychologist?' *Inquiry* 7 (1964), 374–8.

BORTOLASO, G. 'L'analisi del linguaggio secondo L. Wittgenstein.' *Civiltà Cattolica* 109 (Feb. 1958), 268–76.

—. 'Analisi del linguaggio e filosofia.' *Ibid.* 109 (Mar. 1958), 597–605.

—. 'Logica e analisi de linguaggio secondo L. Wittgenstein.' *Ibid.* 109 (Sept. 1958), 495–503.

BOUWSMA, O. K. 'The Blue Book.' *Journal of Philosophy* 58 (1961), 141–62; reprinted in his *Philosophical Essays* (University of Nebraska Press, 1965) and in Fann.

—. 'Wittgenstein Notes, 1949,' unpublished.

BRAITHWAITE, R. B. 'Solipsism and the "Common Sense View of the World".' *Analysis* 1 (1933), 13–5. Comments by M. Cornforth and L. S. Stebbing in *Ibid.*, 21–8.

BRENNAN, JOSEPH G. 'The Philosophy of Language' (with particular reference to Wittgenstein), in his *The Meaning of Philosophy*, 2nd Edition. New York: Harper & Row, 1968.

BRITTON, KARL. 'Portrait of a Philosopher.' *Listener* 53 (June 10th, 1955), 1071–2; reprinted in Fann.

—. 'Recollections of Ludwig Wittgenstein.' *Cambridge Journal* 7 (1954), 709–15.

—. 'Erinnerungen an Wittgenstein.' *Merkur* 11, No. 117 (1957), 1066–72.

—. 'Review of Malcolm's *Memoir*.' *Philosophy* 34 (1959), 277–8.

BROAD, C. D. 'Wittgenstein and the Vienna Circle.' *Mind* 71 (1962), 251.

BROWN, N. O. 'Language and Eros', in his *Life Against Death* (Wesleyan University Press, 1959).

BROWN, STUART. 'Review of Favrholdt.' *Philosophical Quarterly* 16 (1966), 78–9.

BUCHANAN, RUPERT. 'Pictures.' *Dialogos* (Revista del Departmento de Filosofia, Universidad de Puerto Rico) 5 (1968), 130–61.

BUCK, R. C. 'Non-Other Minds', in R. J. Butler (ed.): *Analytical Philosophy* (Oxford: Basil Blackwell, 1962), 187–210.

BUNTING, I. A. 'Some Difficulties in Stenius' Account of the Independence of Atomic States of Affairs.' *Australasian Journal of Philosophy* 43 (1965), 368–75.

BURNHEIM, J. 'Review of *Investigations*.' *Philosophical Studies* (Irish) 4 (1954), 114–5.

BUTCHVAROV, P. 'Meaning-as-Use and Meaning-as-Correspondence.' *Philosophy* 35 (1960), 314–25.

BUTLER, R. J. 'A Wittgensteinian on "The Reality of the Past".' *Philosophical Quarterly* 6 (1956), 304–14.

CAMERON, J. 'The Glass of Language: The Testament of Wittgenstein.' (Review of *Investigations*). *Tablet* 202 (July 4th, 1953), 11–2.

CAMPANALE, D. "II problema dei fondamenti della matematica nella critica di Wittgenstein.' *Rassegna de Scienze Filosofiche* 12 (1959), 18–41.

—. 'La filosofia in Wittgenstein.' *Ibid.* 8 (1955), 417–61.

—. 'Il mondo in Wittgenstein.' *Ibid.* 9 (1956), 38–76.

—. 'La teoria della raffigurazione in Wittgenstein.' *Ibid.* 9 (1956), 159–207.

—. 'Linguaggio ordinario e linguaggio scientifico in *The Blue Book* e in *The Brown Book*.' *Annali della Facoltà di Lettere e Filosofia dell'Univ. di Bari*, 6 (1960), 397–415.

—. 'Investigazioni Filosofiche', in *Dizionario Lettario delle Opere di Tutti i Tempi e di Tutte le Letterature*, Appendice, Vol. 1 (Milano: Bampiania Editrice, 1964).

—. 'Ludwig Wittgenstein', in *Les Grands Courants de la Pensee Contemporaine* (Milano: Marzorati Editrice, 1964), 1525–51.

—. 'L. Wittgenstein: *Tractatus Logico-Philosophicus*.' *Rassegna di Scienze Filosofiche* 7 (1954), 421–8.

CAMPBELL, KEITH. 'Family Resemblance Predicates.' *American Philosophical Quarterly* 2 (1965), 238–44.

CAPPELLETTI, V. 'La Struttura del conoscere secondo L. Wittgenstein.' *La Nuova Critica* 7–8 (1958–59). 47–77.

—. 'L'imperativo del Silenzio. Premessa a Un'interpretazione dell' opera Wittgensteiniana.' *Proceedings of the XII International Congress of Philosophy* (Venice, 1958), XII, 55–61.

CARNAP, RUDOLF. 'Autobiography' in P. Schlipp (ed.): *The Philosophy of Rudolf Carnap* (La Salle, Illinois: Open Court, 1964); an excerpt on Wittgenstein is reprinted in Fann.

CARNEY, JAMES D. 'Is Wittgenstein Impaled on Miss Hervey's Dilemma?' *Philosophy* 38 (1963), 167–9.

—. 'Private Language: The Logic of Wittgenstein's Argument.' *Mind* 69 (1960), 560–5.

CARSE, J. P. 'If a Lion Could talk.' *Theology Today* (Summer, 1967).

CASSIRER, EVA. 'On Logical Structure.' *Proceedings of the Aristotelian Society* 64 (1963–64), 177–98.

—. 'Review of Anscombe.' *British Journal for the Philosophy of Science* 14 (1964), 359–66.

CASTAÑEDA, H. N. 'The Private-Language Argument.' A symposium with comments by Chappell and Thompson, in C. D. Rollins (ed.), 88–125.

—. 'On Mathematical Proofs and Meaning.' *Mind* 70 (1961), 385–90. Criticizes Ambrose (1959).

CAVELL, STANLEY. 'The Availability of Wittgenstein's Later Philosophy.' *Philosophical Review* 71 (1962), 67–93; reprinted in Pitcher.

—. 'Existentialism and Analytic Philosophy.' *Daedalus* 93 (Summer, 1964), 946–74. Section III compares Wittgenstein with Kierkegaard.

CHADWICK, J. A. 'Logical Constants.' *Mind* 36 (1927), 1–11.

CHANDRA, SURESH. 'Wittgenstein's Technique and the Cartesian Doubt.' *Philosophical Quarterly* (India), 33, No. 3 (1960–61).

CHAPPELL, V. C. 'Comments', see under Castañeda.

CHARLESWORTH, M. T. 'Linguistic Analysis and Language About God.' *International Philosophical Quarterly* 1 (1961), 139–57.

CHASTAING, MAXIME. 'Review of *Tractatus*'. *Revue Philosophique* 158 (1968), 133–5.

CHIHARA, CHARLES. 'Mathematical Discovery and Concept Formation.' *Philosophical Review* 72 (1963), 17–34; reprinted in Pitcher.

—. 'Wittgenstein and Logical Compulsion.' *Analysis* 21 (1961), 136–40; reprinted in Pitcher.

CHIHARA, C. S., and J. A. FODOR. 'Operationalism and Ordinary Language: A Critique of Wittgenstein.' *American Philosophical Quarterly* 2 (1965), 281–95; reprinted in Pitcher.

CHIODI, P. 'Essere e linguaggio in Heidegger e nel *Tractatus* di Wittgenstein.' *Rivista de Filosofia* 46 (1955), 170–91.

—. 'Review of Hartnack.' *British Journal for the Philosophy of Science* 15 (1964), 166–8.

CODER, DAVID. 'Family Resemblances and Paradigm Cases.' *Dialogue* 6 (1967), 355–66.

COLLINS, J. 'Review of *Investigations*.' *Thought* 29 (1954), 287–9.

—. 'Review of *Remarks*.' *Modern Schoolman* 35 (1957), 147–50.

—. 'Review of *Lectures and Conversations*.' *Ibid*. 44 (1967), 421–3.

COLOMBO, G. C. M. 'Epilogue on Wittgenstein.' *Month* 18 (1957), 356–8.

—. Letter. *Tablet* (May 15th, 1954), 478. (A reply to Anscombe).

CONTE, AMENDO G. 'L. Wittgenstein: *Tractatus Logico-Philosophicus*.' Tr. Pears and McGuinness. *Rivista de Filofofia* 53 (1962), 92.

—. 'Wittgenstein: *Tractatus Logico-Philosophicus*.' Tr. Pierre Klossowski. *Ibid*. 53 (1962), 222.

—. 'Review of Wittgenstein's *Schriften* and Hartnack.' *Ibid*. 53 (1962), 356–8.

COOK, JOHN W. 'Wittgenstein on Privacy.' *Philosophical Review* 74 (1965), 281–314; reprinted in Pitcher. See Pole.

COOPER, DAVID E. 'The "Fallacies" of Linguistic Philosophy.' *Oxford Review* No. 7 (1968), 79–89. Critical review of Cornforth.

COOPER, NIEL. 'Inconsistency.' *Philosophical Quarterly* 16 (1966), 54–8.

COPELAND, J. W. 'Review of *Investigations*.' *Philosophical Forum* 12 (1954), 112.

COPI, I. M. 'Objects, Properties, and Relations in the *Tractatus*.' *Mind* 67 (1958), 146–65; reprinted in Copi and Beard.

—. 'Review of Stenius.' *Philosophical Review* 72 (1963), 382–90.

—. 'Review of *Notebooks*.' *Journal of Philosophy* 60, (1963), 765–8.

—. '*Tractatus* 5.542.' *Analysis* 18 (1958), 102–4; reprinted in Copi and Beard.

CORNFORTH, MAURICE C. 'The Philosophy of Wittgenstein,' in his *Science and Idealism* (New York: International Publishers, 1947), 141–66.

—. 'A Therapy for Theories,' in his *Marxism and the Linguistic Philosophy* (ibid., 1965), 133–54.

—. 'Review of Hartnack.' *Science and Society* 30 (1966), 335–8.

CORNMAN, JAMES W. 'Private Languages and Private Entities.' *Australasian Journal of Philosophy* 46 (1968).

—. 'Uses of Language and Philosophical Problems.' *Philosophical Studies* 15. Nos. 1–2 (1964), 11–6.

COTRONEO, G. 'Un tentativo di storia di Wittgenstein sui fondamenti della matematica.' *Giornale Critico della Filosofia Italiana* 44 (1965).

COULSON, J. 'Philosophy and Integrity.' (On Wittgenstein and Gellner). *Downside Review* 79 (1961), 122–7.

COUPRIE, D. L. 'Over de Tautologie in Wittgenstein's *Tractatus*.' *Tijdschrift voor Filosofie* (Belgium) 26 (1964), 106–39.

COWAN, J. L. 'Wittgenstein's Philosophy of Logic.' *Philosophical Review* 70 (1961), 362–75; reprinted in Fann.

CRANSTON, MAURICE. 'Bildnis eines Philosophen.' *Monat* 4, No. 41 (1952), 495–7. Reprinted in *Wittgenstein Schriften/-Beiheft*, 16–20.

—. 'L. Wittgenstein.' *World Review* (December, 1951), 21–4. See corrections by Anscombe.

—. 'Vita e morte di Wittgenstein.' *Aut Aut*, No. 9 (Maggio 1952), 239–45.

—. 'Literature of Ideas', in J. Lehmann (ed.): *Craft of Letters in England* (Boston: Houghton Mifflin, 1957), 205–7.

CRITTENDEN, CHARLES. 'Wittgenstein on Philosophical Therapy and Understanding.' *International Philosophical Quarterly* 10 (1970), 20–43.

CUNNINGHAM, G. W. 'Notice of *Investigations*.' *Ethics* 64 (1954), 330.

DAITZ, E. 'The Picture Theory of Meaning.' *Mind* 62 (1953), 184–201; reprinted in A. Flew (ed.): *Essays in Conceptual Analysis* (London: Macmillan & Co., 1964).

DALEY, C. B. 'Polanyi and Wittgenstein.' in Thomas Langford & William Poteat (eds.): *Intellect and Hope: Essays in the Thought of Michael Polanyi* (Duke University Press, 1968), 136–68.

DALY, G. B. 'Logical Positivism, Metaphysics and Ethics, I: Ludwig Wittgenstein.' *Irish Theological Quarterly* 23 (1956), 111–50.

—. 'New Light on Wittgenstein.' *Philosophical Studies* (Irish) Part I: vol. 10 (1960), 5–49; Part II: vol. 11 (1961), 28–62.

—. 'Wittgenstein's "Objects".' *Irish Theological Quarterly* 23 (1956), 413–4.

DAVENPORT, GUY. 'More of Wittgenstein' (review of *Lectures and Conservations* and *Zettel*). *National Review* 20 (March 12th, 1968), 249–52.

DAVIE, I. 'Review of *Investigations*.' *Downside Review* 72 (1954), 119–22.

—. 'Review of *Notebooks*, Anscombe, and Stenius.' *Tablet* 215 (May 6th, 1961), 440.

DAVIS, JOHN W. 'Is Philosophy a Sickness or a Therapy?' *Antioch Review* 23 (1963), 5–23.

DELEDALLE, G. 'Review of *Blue and Brown Books* and *Investigations*,' *Les Études Philosophiques* 14 (1959), 107–8.

DELIUS, HAROLD. 'Was sich überhaupt sagen lasst lasst sich klar sagen. Gedanken zu einer Formulierung Ludwig Wittgensteins.' *Archiv für Philosophie* 8 (1958), 211–54.

DELPECH, LÉON-JACQUES. 'Wittgenstein: Le Cahier Bleu et le Cahier Brun.' *Études Philosophiques* (1965), 562–3.

DIAMOND, CORA. 'Secondary Sense.' *Aristotelian Society Proceedings* 67 (1966–67), 189–208.

DILMAN, ILHAM. 'Imagination.' *Proceedings of the Aristotelian Society*, Suppl. Vol. XLI (1967), 19–36. See Ishiguro.

—. 'Imagination'. *Analysis* 28 (1968), 90–7.

DIVATIA, S. H. 'Language and Philosophy.' *Darshana International* 4 (1964), 78–84.

DONAGAN, A. 'Wittgenstein on Sensation', in Pitcher (ed.), 324–51. See Gustafson (*Analysis*).

DRUDIS BALDRICH, R. 'Ludwig Wittgenstein y su obra filosofica.' *Theoria* (Madrid) 1 (1952), 51–4.

—. 'Consideraciones en torno a la obra de Wittgenstein.' *Revista de Filosofia* (Madrid) 17 (1958), 293–6.

DUBOIS, P. 'Naturaleza della filosofia segundo as "Investigacões filosóficas" de Wittgenstein.' *Revista Portuguesa di Filosofia* 15 (1959), 36–48.

DUFRENNE, MIKEL. 'Wittgenstein et la philosophie.' *Les Études Philosophiques* 20 (1965), 281–306.

—. 'Wittgenstein et Husserl', in his *Jalons* (The Hague: Martinus Nijhoff, 1966), 188–207.

DUMMETT, M. 'Wittgenstein's Philosophy of Mathematics.' *Philosophical Review* 68 (1959), 324–48; reprinted in Pitcher, and in Benacerraf and Putnam (eds.): *Philosophy of Mathematics*.

DUNCAN, A. R. C. 'Wittgenstein,' in *The Architects of Modern Thought*, 3rd Series. A Canadian Broadcasting Co. Publication.

DUTHIE, G. D. 'Critical Study of *Remarks*.' *Philosophical Quarterly* 7 (1957), 368–73.

—. 'Review of Stenius.' *Philosophical Quarterly* 12 (1962), 371–2.

EGIDI, R. 'Due tesi di Wittgenstein sui fondamenti della matematica.' *Giornale Critico della Filosofia Italiana* 44 (Ottobre 1965), 527–38.

EHRLICH, LEONARD H. 'Mystery and Mysticism in Wittgenstein, Aquinas, and Jaspers' (Abstract). *Journal of Philosophy* 64 (1967), 745–6.

EICHNER, HANS. 'Review of the new translation of *Tractatus*'. *Dialogue* 1 (1962), 212–16.

ENGEL, S. MORRIS. 'Reason, Morals and Philosophic Irony.' *Personalist* 45 (1964), 533–55.

—. 'Thought and Language.' *Dialogue* 3 (1964), 160–70.

—. 'Isomorphism and Linguistic Waste.' *Mind* 74 (1965), 28–45.

—. 'Wittgenstein's *Foundations* and Its Reception.' *American Philosophical Quarterly* 4 (1967), 257–68.

—. 'Wittgenstein's *Lectures and Conversations*.' *Dialogue* 6 (1968), 108–21.

—. 'Schopenhauer's Impact on Wittgenstein.' *Journal of the History of Philosophy* 7 (1969), 285–302.

—. 'Wittgenstein and Kant.' *Philos. and Phen. Research* 30 (1970), 483–513.

—. 'Wittgenstein and the Feeling of the Absurd.' *Journal of Existentialism*, forthcoming.

ERNST, C. 'Words, Facts and God; Problems Set by Wittgenstein for Metaphysical Theology.' *Blackfriars* 44 (August 1963), 292–306.

EVANS, E. 'About "aRb".' *Mind* 68 (1959), 535–8; reprinted in Copi and Beard.

—. 'Notes on *Philosophical Investigations*.' *Indian Journal of Philosophy* 2, No. 4 (August 1960), 31–9.

—. 'Tractatus 3.1432.' Mind 64 (1955), 259–60; reprinted in Copi and Beard.

FABRI, ALBRECHT. 'Ludwig Wittgenstein.' Merkur 7 (1953), 1193–6.

FAIRBANKS, MATHEW J. 'C. S. Peirce and Logical Atomism.' New Scholasticism 38 (1964), 178–88. Compares Peirce with Wittgenstein.

—. 'Language-Games and Sensationalism.' Modern Schoolman 40 (1963), 275–81.

FALCK, COLIN. 'Poetry and Wittgenstein.' Review, No. 18 (1968), 3–16.

FANG, J. 'Kant vs. Wittgenstein.' Presented at the International Congress of Philosophy (Vienna, 1968), reprinted in his Kant-Interpretationen, Vol. 2 (W. Germany: Verlag Regensberg), forthcoming.

FARRELL, B. A. 'An Appraisal of Therapeutic Positivism.' I, Mind 55 (1946), 25–48; II, Mind 55 (1946), 133–50.

FAVRHOLDT, D. 'Tractatus 5.542.'' Mind 73 (1964), 557–62.

FEIBLEMAN, J. K. 'A Commentary to the Tractatus,' in his Inside the Great Mirror, 51–129.

—. 'Reflections after Wittgenstein's Philosophical Investigations.' Sophia 23 (1955); reprinted in his Inside the Great Mirror, 203–16.

FERRATER MORA, JOSÉ. 'Wittgenstein, simbolo de una epoca angustiada.' Theoria (Madrid) 2 (1954), 33–8.

—. 'Wittgenstein, A Symbol of Troubled Times.' Philos. and Pheno. Research 14 (1953), 89–96; reprinted in Fann.

—. 'Wittgenstein o la destruccion.' Realidad (Buenos Aires) 3, No. 14 (1949), 129–40.

—. 'Wittgenstein oder die Destruktion.' Monat 4, No. 41 (1952); reprinted in Wittgenstein: Schriften/Beiheft, 21–9.

—. 'Del uso.' Dialogos 5 (1968), 61–78.

FERRÉ, F. 'Colour Incompatibility and Language Games.' Mind 70 (1961), 90–4. See Swiggart.

FEYERABEND, PAUL. 'Ludwig Wittgenstein.' Merkur 8 (1954), 1021–38; reprinted in Wittgenstein: Schriften/Beiheft, 30–47.

—. 'Review of Specht.' *Philosophical Quarterly* 16 (1966), 79–80.

—. 'Wittgenstein und die Philosophie.' *Wissenschaft und Weltbild* 7 (1954), 212–20; 283–92.

—. 'Wittgenstein's *Philosophical Investigations*.' *Philosophical Review* 64 (1955), 449–83; reprinted in Pitcher and in Fann.

FEYS, R. 'Le raissonement en Termes de faits dans la Logistique Russellienne.' *Revue Neo-Scholastique de Philosophie* 29 (1927), 393–421; 30 (1928), 154–92; 257–74.

FICKER, L. 'Rilke und der unbekannte Freund.' *Der Brenner* 18 (1954), 234–48.

FINDLAY, J. N. 'Wittgenstein's *Philosophical Investigations*.' *Philosophy* 30 (1955), 173–9; reprinted in his *Language, Mind and Value* (New York: Humanities Press, 1963).

—. 'Wittgenstein's Philosophical Investigations.' *Revue Internationale de Philosophie* 7 (1953), 201–16.

—. 'Some Reactions to Recent Cambridge Philosophy.' *Australasian Journal of Psychology and Philosophy* 18 (1940), 193–211; 19 (1941), 1–13.

FITZPATRICK, P. 'Review of *The Blue and Brown Books*.' *Tablet* 212 (Nov. 29, 1958), 482.

FLEMING, NOEL. 'Recognizing and Seeing As.' *Philosophical Review* 66 (1957), 161–79.

FLEW, A. 'The *Tractatus*' (review of Black). *Spectator* 213 (Nov. 13th, 1964), 640.

—. 'Review of *Lectures and Conversations*.' *Spectator* (Sept. 16th, 1966), 355.

FODER, JERRY A. and JERROLD KATZ. 'The Availability of What we Say.' *Philosophical Review* 72 (1963), 57–71. Comments on Cavell's article.

FØLLESDAL, DAGFINN. 'Comments on Stenius' "Mood and Language-Game".' *Synthese* 17 (1967), 275–80.

FRAYN, MICHAEL. 'Russell and Wittgenstein.' *Commentary* 43, No. 5 (May 1967), 68–75.

FREUNDLICH, R. 'Logic und Mystik.' *Zeitschrift für Philosophische Forschung* 7 (1953), 554–70.

FRICK, I. E. 'Whitehead and "Ordinary Language" Philosophers.' *Indian Journal of Philosophy* 4 (1964), 69–84.

FUNKE, GERHARD. 'Einheitssprache, Sprachspiel und Sprachauslegung bei Wittgenstein.' *Zeitschrift für Philosophische Forschung* 22 (1968), 1–30, and 216–47.

G. N. (signed by). 'Ludwig Wittgenstein (1889–1951).' *Vijsg. Persp. Maatsch. Wet*, 1 (1960–61), 246–50.

GABRIEL, L. 'Logische Magie. Ein Nachwort zum Thema Wittgenstein.' *Wissenschaft und Weltbild* 7 (1954), 288–93.

GAHRINGER, R. E. 'Can Games Explain Language?' *Journal of Philosophy* 56 (1959), 661–7.

GALE, RICHARD M. 'Review of Copi and Beard.' *Phil. and Pheno. Research* 29 (1968), 146–7.

GALLAGHER, M. P. 'Wittgenstein's Admiration for Kierkegaard.' *Month* 39 (1968), 43–9.

GARDINER, PATRICK. 'Schopenhauer and Wittgenstein,' in his *Schopenhauer* (London: Penguin Books, 1963), 275–82.

GARELLI, JAQUES. 'Wittgenstein et l'analyse du langage.' *Les Temps Modernes* 18 (1963), 2268–78.

GARGANI, A. G. 'Linguaggio e societa in Moore e Wittgenstein.' *Giornale Critico della Filosofia Italiana* 44 (Genn-Marzo, 1965).

GARVER, NEWTON. 'Review of *Blue and Brown Books*.' *Philos. and Pheno. Research* 21 (1961), 576–7.

—. 'Review of Stenius.' *Ibid.* 22 (1962), 276–7.

—. 'Criteria of Personal Identity.' *Journal of Philosophy* 61 (1964), 779–84.

—. 'Wittgenstein on Criteria.' A symposium with comments by Ginet, Siegler, and Ziff; in Rollins, 55–87.

—. 'Wittgenstein on Private Language.' *Philos. and Pheno. Research* 20 (1960), 389–96.

GASKING, D. A. T. 'Anderson and the *Tractatus*.' *Australasian Journal of Philosophy* 27 (1949), 1–26.

—. 'Avowals', in R. J. Butler (ed.): *Analytical Philosophy* (Oxford: Basil Blackwell, 1962), 154–69.

—. and A. C. Jackson. 'Ludwig Wittgenstein', a memorial notice. *Australasian Journal of Philosophy* 29 (1951), 73–80; reprinted in Fann as 'Wittgenstein as a Teacher'.

GASS, WILLIAM H. 'Wittgenstein—A man and a half.' *New Republic* 158 (June 22nd, 1968), 29–30. (Review of Engelmann. Includes a reminiscence of Wittgenstein in a meeting of the Cornell Philosophical Club).

GEACH, P. T. 'Review of Colombo's Italian translation of *Tractatus*.' *Philosophical Review* 66 (1957), 556–9.

—. 'Review of *Tractatus* as translated into English by Pears and McGuinness.' *Ibid*. 72 (1963), 264–5.

—. 'Wittgenstein's Alleged Rejection of Mental Acts', in his *Mental Acts* (London: Routledge & Kegan Paul, 1957), 2–4.

GERT, BERNARD. 'Wittgenstein and Logical Positivism' (abstract). *Journal of Philosophy* 57 (1961), 707.

—. 'Wittgenstein and Private Language' (abstract). *Ibid*. 61 (1964), 700.

GIACOMINI, UGO. 'Appunti Sull'etica di Wittgenstein.' *Aut Aut*, No. 91 (Gennaio, 1966), 72–80.

—. 'Il problema del linguaggio nella seconda ricerca filosofica di Wittgenstein.' *Ibid*. No. 69 (Maggio, 1962), 238–44.

—. 'Wittgenstein oggi.' *Ibid*. No. 71 (Settembre 1962), 415–9.

—. 'Interpretazioni del *Tractatus* di Wittgenstein.' *Ibid*. No. 73 (Gennaio 1963), 63–75.

—. 'Un'opera architettonica di Wittgenstein.' *Ibid*. No. 87 Maggio (1965), 88–92. On the Stonborough villa which Wittgenstein built. Pictures of the villa and a sculpture he made are included.

GILL, JERRY H. 'Review of Hartnack and Anscombe.' *Philos. and Pheno. Research* 27 (1966), 137–8.

—. 'Wittgenstein and Religious Language.' *Theology Today* 21 (1964), 59–72.

—. 'Wittgenstein's Concept of Truth.' *International Philosophical Quarterly* 6 (1966), 71–80.

—. 'Wittgenstein on the Use of "I".' *Southern Journal of Philosophy* 5 (1967), 26–35.

—. 'Wittgenstein's *Philosophical Investigations*: An Annotated Table of Contents." *International Philosophical Quarterly* 7 (1967), 305–10.

—. 'God-Talk: Getting on with It. A Review of Current Literature.' *Southern Journal of Philosophy* 6 (1968), 115–24.

GINET, CARL. 'How Words Mean Kinds of Sensations.' *Philosophical Review* 77 (1968), 3–24.

—. 'Comments,' see under Garver.

GOFF, ROBERT A. 'The Wittgenstein Game.' *Christian Scholar* 45, No. 3 (Fall, 1962).

GOLDBERG, BRUCE. 'The Correspondence Hypothesis.' *Philosophical Review* 77 (1968), 438–54.

GOLFFING, FRANCIS. 'Review of Wittgenstein's *Schriften*.' *Books Abroad* 36 (Autumn, 1962), 405.

GOODSTEIN, R. L. 'Critical Notice of *Remarks*.' *Mind* 66 (1957), 549–53.

GOSSELIN, M. 'Enkele Beschouwingen naar aanleiding van "Language as Hermeneutic in the Later Wittgenstein" ' (With Kerr's reply). *Tijdschrift voor Filosofie* 28 (1966), 74–83.

GOURLIE, JOHN. 'Findlay on *Words and Things*.' *Indian Journal of Philosophy* 4 (1964), 56–61. Criticizes Findlay and Gellner's criticisms of Wittgenstein.

GREGORY, T. S. 'Mere Words? Wittgenstein and the Care of Language.' *Tablet* 203 (April 10th, 1954), 343–5.

GRIFFIN, JAMES. 'Review of Black.' *Philosophical Books* 6 (1965), 2–4.

—. 'Review of Pitcher and Favrholdt.' *Mind* 74 (1965), 438–41.

GRUENDER, D. 'Wittgenstein on Explanation and Description.' *Journal of Philosophy* 59 (1962), 523–30.

—. 'Language, Society, and Knowledge.' *Antioch Review* 28 (1968), 187–212.

144   BIBLIOGRAPHY

GUSTAFSON, D. F. 'Privacy.' *Southern Journal of Philosophy* 3 (1965), 140–6.
—. 'On Pitcher's Account of *Investigations* §43.' *Philos. and Pheno. Research* 28 (1967), 252–8.
—. 'Review of *Zettel.*' *Philosophy* 43 (1968), 161–4.
—. 'A Note on A Misreading of Wittgenstein'. *Analysis* 28 (1968), 143–4. Comments on Donagan.
HABERMAS, JÜRGEN. 'Zur Logic de Sozialwissenschaften.' *Philosophische Rundschau* Beiheft 5 (1967), 124ff.
HACKSTAFF, L. H. 'A Note on Wittgenstein's Truth-Function-Generating Operation in *Tractatus* 6.' *Mind* 75 (1966), 255–6.
HADOT, P. 'Réflexions sur les limites du langage à propos du *Tractatus logico-philosophicus* de Wittgenstein.' *Revue de Métaphysique et de Morale* 64 (1959), 469–84.
—. 'Wittgenstein, Philosophe du Langage.' *Critique*, Nos. 149 (1959), 866–81 and 150 (1959), 972–83.
—. 'Jeux de Langage et Philosophie.' *Revue de Métaphysique et de Morale* 67 (1962), 330–43.
HALBOROW, L. C. 'Wittgenstein's Kind of Behaviorism?' *Philosophical Quarterly* 17 (1967), 345–57.
HALL, ROLAND. 'Review of *Philosophical Investigations*, 3rd Edition.' *Philosophical Quarterly* 17 (1967), 362–3.
HALLIE, PHILIP P. 'Wittgenstein's Grammatical-Empirical Distinction'. *Journal of Philosophy* 60 (1963), 565–78.
—. 'Wittgenstein's Exclusion of Metaphysical Nonsense.' *Philosophical Quarterly* 16 (1966), 97–112.
HAMBURG, CARL. 'Whereof One Cannot Speak.' *Journal of Philosophy* 50 (1953), 662–4.
HAMILTON, R. 'Review of *Investigations.*' *Month* 11 (1954), 116–7.
HAMLYN, D. W. 'Categories, Formal Concepts and Metaphysics.' *Philosophy* 34 (1959), 111–24.
—. 'The Correspondence Theory of Truth.' *Philosophical Quarterly* 12 (1962), 193–205.
HAMPSHIRE, STUART. 'Out of the World.' A review of

Philosophische Bemerkungen. New Statesmen 71 (Feb. 4th, 1966), 163–4.

—. 'The Proper Method.' A review of *The Blue and Brown Books. Ibid.* 56 (Aug. 23rd, 1958), 228–9.

—. 'A Great Philosopher.' A review of the *Investigations. Spectator* 190 (May 22nd, 1953), 682.

HANNAY, ALASTAIR. 'Was Wittgenstein a Psychologist?' *Inquiry* 7 (1964), 379–86.

HARDIN, C. L. 'Wittgenstein on Private Language.' *Journal of Philosophy* 56 (1959), 513–28.

HARDWICK, CHARLES S. 'Doing Philosophy and Doing Zen.' *Philosophy East and West* 13 (1963), 227–34. (Compares Wittgenstein and Zen.)

HARRIS, ROY. 'The Semantics of Self-Description.' *Analysis* 27 (1967), 144. (On *Tractatus* 3.332).

HARRISON, FRANK R. 'Notes on Wittgenstein's use of "das Mystische".' *Southern Journal of Philosophy* 1 (1963), 3–9.

—. 'Wittgenstein and the Doctrine of Identical Minimal Meaning.' *Methodos* 14 (1962), 61–74.

HAWKINS, BEN. 'Note on a Doctrine of Frege and Wittgenstein.' *Mind*, 75 (1966), 583–5.

HAWKINS, D. J. B. 'Wittgenstein and the Cult of Language.' *Aquinas Paper* No. 27 (London: Blackfriars Publications, 1956); reprinted in his *Crucial Problems of Modern Philosophy* (University of Notre Dame Press, 1962), 66–79.

HEATH, P. L. 'Wittgenstein Investigated.' *Philosophical Quarterly* 6 (1956), 66–71.

HEINEMANN, F. H. 'Review of *Philosophical Investigations.*' *Hibbert Journal* 52 (1953), 89–90.

HELLER, ERICH. 'L. Wittgenstein: Unphilosophical Notes.' *Encounter* 13 (Sept., 1959), 40–8; reprinted in his *An Artist's Journey into the Interior and other Essays* (New York: Random House, 1965), and in Fann. German version appeared in *Merkur* 13, No. 142 (1958), and in *Wittgenstein: Schriften/Beiheft.*

HENNEMANN, GERHARD. 'Review of Hartnack.' *Zeitschrift für philosophische Forschung* 20 (1966), 338–41.

HENRY, GRANVILLE C. JR., 'Aspects of the Influence of Mathematics on Contemporary Philosophy.' *Philosophia Mathematica* 3 (1966), 17–37. (A section on Wittgenstein).

HERMANS, W. F. 'Wittgenstein in de Mode.' *Algemeen Nederlands Tijdschrift voor Wijsbegeerte en Psychologie* 58 jaargang (December 1966).

HERVEY, HELEN. 'The Private Language Problem.' *Philosophical Quarterly* 7 (1957), 63–79.

—. 'The Problem of the Model Language Game in Wittgenstein's Later Philosophy.' *Philosophy* 36 (1961), 333–51.

—. 'A Reply to Dr. Carney's Challenge.' *Philosophy* 38 (1963), 170–5.

HESTER, M. B. 'Metaphor and Aspect Seeing.' *Journal of Aesthetics and Art Criticism* 25 (1966), 205–12.

—. 'Wittgenstein's Analysis of "I Know I am in Pain".' *Southern Journal of Philosophy* 4 (1966), 274–9.

HINTIKKA, JAAKKO. 'Are Logical Truths Analytic?' *Philosophical Review* 74 (1965), 178–203.

—. 'Identity, Variables and Impredicative Definitions.' *Journal of Symbolic Logic* 21 (1957), 225–45.

—. 'On Wittgenstein's "Solipsism".' *Mind* 67 (1958), 88–91.

HOFFMAN, ROBERT. 'Logic, Meaning and Mystical Situation.' *Philosophical Studies* 11 (1960), 65–70.

HOPE, V. M. 'Wittgenstein and Self-description.' *Inquiry* 11 (1968).

HORGBY, I. 'The Double Awareness in Heidegger and Wittgenstein.' *Inquiry* 2 (1959), 235–64. See Weil.

HUBY, P. M. 'Family Resemblance.' *Philosophical Quarterly* 18 (1968), 66–7. Criticizes Pompa's article.

HUDSON, W. D. 'On Two Points Against Wittgenstein Fideism.' *Philosophy* 43 (1968), 269–73. See Nielsen.

HUNTER, JOHN. 'Review of Griffin.' *Dialogue* 3 (1965), 461–2.

—. 'Review of Pitcher.' *Ibid.* (1965), 463–4.

—. 'Wittgenstein's Theory of Linguistic Self-Sufficiency.' *Ibid.* 6 (1967), 367–78.

HUTTEN, E. H. 'Review of *Investigations*.' *British Journal for the Philosophy of Science* 4 (1953), 258–60.

IRVING, J. A. 'Mysticism and the Limits of Communication,' in A. Stiernotte (ed.), *Mysticism and the Modern World* (New York: Liberal Arts Press, 1959).

ISHIGURO, HIDÉ. 'Imagination'. *Proceedings of the Aristotelian Society*, Supp. Vol. XLI (1967), 37–56. A reply to Dilman.

JACOB, ANDRE. 'Review of the *Tractatus*.' *Les Études Philosophiques* 16 (1961), 477.

JARVIS, J. 'Professor Stenius on the *Tractatus*.' *Journal of Philosophy* 58 (1961), 584–96; reprinted in Copi and Beard.

—. 'Review of the new translation of *Tractatus*.' *Journal of Philosophy* 59 (1962), 332–5.

—. and F. SOMMERS 'Review of Anscombe.' *Philosophy* 36 (1961), 374–6.

J[OHANSON], A. E. 'Notice of Favrholdt.' *Review of Metaphysics* 20 (1966), 150.

JONES, J. R. 'How Do I Know Who I Am?' *Proceedings of the Aristotelian Society*, Suppl. Vol. XLI (1967), 1–18.

JÖRGENSEN, JÖRGEN. 'L. Wittgenstein's Logical-Philosophical Treatise', in his *Development of Logical Empiricism* (University of Chicago Press, 1951).

JÜNGER, F. G. 'Satzsinn und Satzbedeutung. Gedanken zu den "Schriften" von Ludwig Wittgenstein.' *Merkur* 15 (1961), 1009–23; reprinted in his *Sprache und Denken* (Frankfurt/M., 1962).

KATZ, JERROLD J. 'Ordinary Language Philosophy', in his *Philosophy of Language* (New York: Harper & Row, 1966), 68–93.

KAUFMANN, FELIX. 'Basic Issues in Logical Positivism', in M. Farber (ed.): *Philosophic Thought in France and the United States* (Buffalo University Press, 1950).

KAUFMANN, WALTER. 'Wittgenstein' and 'Wittgenstein and Socrates', in his *Critique of Religion and Philosophy* (New York: Harper & Row, 1958), 52–9.

KAZEMIER, B. H. 'Wittgenstein in het Geding (I).' *Algemeen Nederlands Tijdschrift voor Wijsbegeerte en psychologie* 58 (December 1966).

KEMPSKI, JÜRGEN VON. 'Über Wittgenstein.' *Neue Deutsche Hefte* 82 (1961), 43–60.

—. 'Wittgenstein und Analytische Philosophie.' *Merkur* 15 (1961), 664–76.

—. 'Anotaciones sobre Wittgenstein.' *Dialogos* 5 (1968), 101–14.

—. 'Wittgenstein y la filosofia analitica.' *Ibid.*, 115–29.

KENNY, A. 'Cartesian Privacy', in Pitcher (ed.), 352–70.

—. 'Aquinas and Wittgenstein.' *Downside Review* 77 (1959), 217–35. See Williams.

—. 'Review of Black,' *Mind* 75 (1966), 452–3.

KENT, EDWARD. 'Justice as Respect for Person.' *Southern Journal of Philosophy* 6 (1968), 70–7.

KERR, F. 'Language as Hermeneutic in the Later Wittgenstein.' *Tijdschrift voor Filosofie* 27 (1965), 491–520. See Gosselin.

—. 'Reply to Gosselin.' *Ibid.* 28 (1966).

KEYSER, C. J. 'A Short Notice of Wittgenstein's *Tractatus*.' *Bulletin of the American Mathematical Society* 30 (March–April, 1924), 179–81.

KEYT, DAVID. 'A New Interpretation of the *Tractatus* Examined.' *Philosophical Review* 74 (1965), 229–39.

—. 'Wittgenstein's Notion of an Object.' *Philosophical Quarterly* 13 (1963), 13–25; reprinted in Copi and Beard.

—. 'Wittgenstein's Picture Theory of Language.' *Philosophical Review* 73 (1964), 493–511; reprinted in Copi and Beard.

KHATCHADOURIAN, HAIG. 'Common Names and Family Resemblances.' *Philos. and Pheno. Research* 18 (1958), 341–58; reprinted in Pitcher.

KING-FARLOW, JOHN. 'Postscript to Mr. Aune on a Wittgensteinian Dogma.' *Philosophical Studies* 13 (1962), 62–3.

KLAWONN, ERICH. 'Criteria and Private Language.' *Danish Yearbook of Philosophy* 3 (1966), 29–54.

KNEALE, WILLIAM. 'Truths of Logic.' *Proceedings of the Aristotelian Society* 46 (1945–6), 207–34.

KOHL, HERBERT. 'Wittgenstein Returns', in his *The Age of Complexity* (A Mentor book, 1965), 119–28.

KOLENDA, K. 'Wittgenstein's "Weltanschauung".' *Rice University Studies* 50, No. 1 (*Papers in Philosophy*, 1961), 23–37.

KOZLOVA, M. S. 'Logic and Reality: Critical Analysis of Wittgenstein's Conception of Logical Reflection of Reality in his *Tractatus*.' *Voprosy Filosofii* (1965, No. 9), 95–105. (In Russian with an English summary.)

KOZY, JOHN JR. 'A New Look at Linguistic Analysis'. *Southern Journal of Philosophy* 5 (1967), 155–9.

KRAFT, V. 'Ludwig Wittgenstein.' *Wiener Zeitschrfit für Philosophie, Psychologie, Pädagogik* 3, Heft 3 (1951), 161–3.

KRAFT, WERNER. 'Ludwig Wittgenstein und Karl Kraus.' *Die Neue Rundschau* 72 (1961), 812–44.

KREISEL, G. 'Wittgenstein's *Remarks*.' (With Anscombe's corrections to her translation.) *British Journal for the Philosophy of Science* 9 (1958), 135–58.

—. 'Wittgenstein's Theory and Practice of Philosophy.' *British Journal for the Philosophy of Science* 11 (1960), 238–52.

KRETZMANN, NORMAN. 'Maupertius, Wittgenstein, and the Origin of Language' (abstract). *Journal of Philosophy* 54 (1957), 776.

KULTGEN, J. H. 'Can There Be a Public Language?' *Southern Journal of Philosophy* 6 (1968), 31–44.

KUNTZ, P. G. 'Order in Language, Phenomena, and Reality: Notes on Linguistic Analysis, Phenomenology and Metaphysics.' *Monist* 49 (1965), 107–36.

KURTZ, P. W. 'Letter to the Editor Concerning Wittgenstein's *Notes on Logic*.' *Journal of Philosophy* 59 (1962), 78–9.

KUTSCHERA, FRANZ V. 'Review of Griffin.' *Philosophische Rundschau* 12 (Jan. 1965), 291–5.

LAGUNA, THEODORE DE. 'Review of *Tractatus*.' *Philosophical Review* 33 (1924), 103–9; reprinted in Copi and Beard.

LANGFORD, C. H. 'On Propositions Belonging to Logic.' *Mind* 36 (1927), 342–6.

LAYCOCK, H. 'Ordinary Language and Materialism.' *Philosophy* 42 (1967), 363–7.

LÁZARO, RAMÓN CASTILLA. 'Lenguaje y Ontología. En torno al Wittgenstein de E. K. Specht.' *Dialogos* 5 (1968), 79–100.

LAZEROWITZ, MRS. MORRIS, see under Ambrose, Alice.

LAZEROWITZ, MORRIS. 'Wittgenstein on the Nature of Philosophy,' Part I of his joint paper with Ambrose in Mace (ed.): *British Philosophy in Mid-Century*, (1966 revised edition), 155–74; reprinted in Fann.

—. 'Tautologies and the Matrix Method.' *Mind* 46 (1937), 191–205.

—. 'Tiempo Y Terminologia Temporal.' *Dialogos* 5 (1968), 7–34.

LEVI, ALBERT W. 'G. E. Moore and Ludwig Wittgenstein', in his *Philosophy and Modern World* (Indiana University Press, 1959), 436–81.

—. 'Wittgenstein as Dialectician.' *Journal of Philosophy* 61 (1964), 127–39; reprinted in Fann.

LEVISON, A. B. 'Wittgenstein and Logical Laws.' *Philosophical Quarterly* 14 (1964), 345–54; revised and combined version of this and the following article is reprinted in Fann.

—. 'Wittgenstein and Logical Necessity.' *Inquiry* 7 (1964), 367–73.

LEWIS, C. J. 'Review of *Remarks*.' *Thought* 32 (1957), 446–8.

LEWY, C. 'A Note on the Text of the *Tractatus*.' *Mind* 76 (1967), 416–23.

LIEB, IRWIN C. 'Wittgenstein's Investigations.' *Review of Metaphysics* 8 (1954), 125–43.

LINSKY, L. 'Meaning and Use.' *Algemeen Nederlands Tijdschrift voor Wijsbegeerte en Psychologie*, 53 (1960), 201–7.

—. 'Wittgenstein on Language and Some Problems of Philosophy.' *Journal of Philosophy* 54 (1957), 285–93; reprinted in Fann.

LLEWELYN, J. E. 'On Not Speaking the Same Language.' *Australasian Journal of Philosophy* 40 (1962), 35–48 and 127–45.

—. 'Family Resemblance.' *Philosophical Quarterly* 18 (1968), 344–6. Criticism of Pompa.

LONG, T. A. 'The Problem of Pain and Contextual Implication.' *Philos. and Pheno. Research* 26 (1965), 106–11.

—. 'Two Conceptions of Wittgensteinian Criteria.' *Philosophical Quarterly* (India), 39 (1966), 81–96.

LORENZEN, PAUL. 'Notice of *Blue and Brown Books*.' *Philosophische Rundschau* 7 (1959), 160.

LOWENFELS, WALTER. 'For Ludwig Wittgenstein (1880–1951),' A Poem. *ETC*. (A Review of General Semantics) 22 (1965), 164.

LÜBBE, HERMANN. ' "Sprachspiele" und "Geschichten".' *Kant-Studien* 52 (1960/61), 220–43.

—. 'Wittgenstein—ein Existentialist?' *Philosophische Jahrbuch* 69 (1962), 311–24,

'Ludwig Wittgenstein: A Symposium', by Erich Heller, M. O'C. Drury. Norman Malcolm and Rush Rhees. *Listener* 63 (Jan. 28th, 1960), 163–5; and 63 (Feb. 4th, 1960), 207–9; reprinted in Fann.

'Ludwig Wittgenstein.' See the various entries in Paul Edwards (ed.): *The Encyclopedia of Philosophy*, 8 vols.

'Ludwig Wittgenstein', in E. Gilson, T. Langan and A. A. Maurer: *Recent Philosophy* (New York: Random House, 1962), 521–30.

LUGTON, ROBERT C. 'Ludwig Wittgenstein: The Logic of Language.' *ETC* 22 (1965), 165–92.

MACGREGOR, G. 'Notice of the *Tractatus*.' *Personalist* 43 (1962), 559.

MACINTYRE, ALASDAIR. 'Guide Through a Maze.' (Review of Black.) *Guardian* (Oct. 23rd, 1964), 13.

MACIVOR, COLIN. 'The Importance of Wittgenstein.' A letter replying to Smiley. *Tablet* 203 (Feb., 6th, 1954), 140.

MALCOLM, N. 'Knowledge of Other Minds.' *Journal of*

Philosophy 55 (1958), 969–78. Reprinted in Chappell (ed.): *Philosophy of Mind* (Prentice-Hall, 1962); in Malcolm: *Knowledge and Certainty*; and in Pitcher.

—. 'Wittgenstein's *Philosophical Investigations.*' *Philosophical Review* 63 (1954), 530–59; reprinted in Chappell (ed.): *Philosophy of Mind*; in Malcolm: *Knowledge and Certainty*; in Pitcher, in Fann, and in Morick.

—. 'Wittgenstein's *Philosophische Bemerkungen.*' *Philosophical Review* 76 (1967), 220–9.

—. 'Ludwig Josef Johann Wittgenstein', in Paul Edwards (ed.): *The Encyclopedia of Philosophy*, Vol. 8, 327–40.

—. 'The Privacy of Experience', in Avrum Stroll (ed.): *Epistemology: New Essays in the Theory of Knowledge* (New York: Harper & Row, 1967), 129–58.

—. 'Wittgenstein on the Nature of Mind.' An Isenberg Lecture. *American Philosophical Quarterly* Monograph No. 4 (1970), 9–29.

MANDELBAUM, MAURICE. 'Family Resemblances and Generalization Concerning the Arts.' *American Philosophical Quarterly* 2 (1965), 219–28.

—. 'Language and Chess: De Saussure's Analogy.' *Philosophical Review* 77 (1968), 356–7.

MANSER, A. R. 'Games and Family Resemblances.' *Philosophy* 42 (1967), 210–24.

MARCUSE, HERBERT. 'The Triumph of Positive Thinking: One-Dimensional Philosophy', in his *One-Dimensional Man* (Boston: Beacon Press, 1961), 170–202.

MARDIROS, A. M. 'Shapers of the Modern Outlook—Ludwig Wittgenstein: Philosopher.' *Canadian Forum* 33 (Jan. 1954), 223–5.

MARGOLIS, JOSEPH. 'The Privacy of Sensation.' *Ratio* 6 (1964), 147–53.

—. 'The Problem of Criteria of Pain.' *Dialogue* 4 (1956), 62–71.

MASLOW, ALEXANDER. 'Letters to the Editors.' A reply to R. Rhees. *Philosophical Review* 73 (1964), 290.

MATHRANI, G. N. 'A Comparative and Critical Study of Wittgenstein's and Ayer's Theories of Meaning.' *Philosophical Quarterly* (India) 37 (Jan. 1965), 219–26.

MAYS, W. 'Note on Wittgenstein's Manchester Period.' *Mind* 64 (1955), 247–8.

—. 'Recollections of Wittgenstein,' in Fann, 79–88.

—. 'Wittgenstein's Manchester Period.' *Guardian* (March 24, 1961); reprinted in Fann.

MCBRIEN, V. O. 'Review of *Remarks*' *New Scholasticism* 32 (1958), 269–71.

MCCALL, STORRS. 'Review of Maslow.' *Dialogue* 2 (1963), 114–5.

MCCLOSKEY, A. J. 'The Philosophy of Linguistic Analysis and the Problem of Universals.' *Philos. and Pheno. Research* 24 (1964), 329–38.

MCGILL, V. F. 'An Evaluation of Logical Positivism.' *Science and Society* 1 (1936–7), 45–80.

MCGUINNESS, B. F. 'Pictures and Forms in Wittgenstein's *Tractatus*', in E. Castelli (ed.): *Filosofia e Simbolismo, Archivio di Filosofia* (Roma), Nos. 2–3, (1956), 207–28. Italian translation follows, 229–47.

—. 'The Mysticism of the *Tractatus*.' *Philosophical Review* 75 (1966), 305–28.

MCMULLIN, ERNAN. 'The Analytical Approach to Philosophy.' *Proceedings of the American Catholic Philosophical Association* 34 (1960), 80–109.

MCTAGGART, J. E. 'Propositions Applicable to Themselves.' *Mind* 32 (1923), 462–4.

MEHTA, VED. 'A Battle Against the Bewitchment of Our Intelligence', *New Yorker* (Dec. 9th, 1961), 59–159. Reprinted in his *The Fly and the Fly Bottle: Encounters with British Intellectuals* (Boston: Little, Brown & Company, 1962).

MEILAND, J. W. 'Analogy, Verification and Other Minds.' *Mind* 75 (1966), 564–8.

MELDEN, A. I. 'My Kinaesthetic Sensations Advise Me . . .' *Analysis* 18 (1957), 43–8.

MELLOR, W. W. 'Three Problems About Other Minds.' *Mind* 65 (1956), 200–17.

MEYER, H. 'La Philosophie de L. Wittgenstein.' *Algemeen Nederlands Tijdschrift voor Wijsbegeerte en Psychologie* 48 (1956), 44–53.

—. 'Zin en Onzin volgens L. Wittgenstein.' *Ibid.* 48 (1956), 202–8.

MILLER, J. 'Wittgenstein's Weltanschauung.' *Philosophical Studies* (Irish), 13 (1964), 127–40.

MILLER, ROBERT G. 'Linguistic Analysis and Metaphysics.' *Proceedings of the American Catholic Philosophical Association* 34 (1960), 80–109.

MILLS, JOHN F. 'A Meeting with Wittgenstein.' *Times Lit. Suppl.* (June 12th, 1959), 353.

MOJTABAI, A. G. 'Linguistic Analysis and Religious Language.' *Philosophy Today* 2 (1967), 60–71.

MOOD, J. J. 'Poetic Languaging and Primal Thinking; A Study of Barfield, Wittgenstein, and Heidegger.' *Encounter* 26 (1965), 417–33.

MOORE, G. E. 'An Autobiography', in P. Schilpp (ed.): *The Philosophy of G. E. Moore* (Evanston, Illinois: Open Court, 1942). An excerpt on Wittgenstein reprinted in Fann.

—. 'Truth Possibilities', and 'Wittgenstein's Sense of "Tautology",' in his *Commonplace Book* (London: George Allen & Unwin, 1962), 282–6.

—. 'Wittgenstein's Lectures in 1930–33.' See (I) above.

MOORE, WILLIS. 'Structure in Sentence and in Fact.' *Philosophy of Science* 5 (1938), 81–8; reprinted in Copi and Beard.

MORICK, HAROLD. 'Logically Private Ownership and Epistemic Privilege—A Critique of Wittgenstein' (abstract). *Journal of Philosophy* 43 (1966), 583.

VON MORSTEIN, PETRA. 'Erfahrung bei Ludwig Wittgenstein.' *Archiv für Philosophie* 12 (1963), 133–51.

—. 'Philosophie-Verwalterin der Grammatik über die Schriften des "mittleren" Wittgenstein.' (Review of *Philosophische Bemerkungen*). *Die Welt: Der Literatur* 2, No. 9 (April 29th, 1965), 216.

—. 'Wittgenstein's Untersuchungen des Wortes, "Schmerz".' *Archiv für Philosophie* 13 (1964), 132–40.

MOSS, J. M. B. 'Review of Pitcher.' *Philosophical Books* 6 (1956), 20–3.

MUKHERJA, S. R. 'The Problem of Other Minds.' *Philosophical Quarterly* (India) 39 (1966), 19–25.

MUNDLE, C. W. K. ' "Private Language" and Wittgenstein's kind of Behaviorism.' *Philosophical Quarterly* 16 (1966), 35–46.

MUNSON, T. N. 'Wittgenstein's Phenomenology.' *Philos. and Pheno. Research* 23 (1962), 37–50.

MUNZ, PETER. 'Popper and Wittgenstein', in M. A. Bunge (ed.): *The Critical Approach to Science and Philosophy* (New York: Free Press, 1964), 82–91.

NAGEL, ERNEST. 'Impressions and Appraisals of Analytic Philosophy in Europe.' *Journal of Philosophy* 33 (1936), 5–53.

NAKHNIKIAN, GEORGE. 'Review of *Investigations*.' *Philosophy of Science* 12 (1954), 253–4.

NARVESON, ANNE. 'Black's *A Companion to the Tractatus*.' *Philosophy of Science* 34 (1967), 69–73.

—. 'Review of Pitcher.' *Ibid.* 34 (1967), 80–3.

—. 'Review of Hartnack.' *Dialogue* 5 (1966), 101–2.

—. 'The Ontology of the *Tractatus*.' *Ibid.* 3 (1964), 273–83.

NELL, EDWARD. 'The Hardness of the Logical "Must".' *Analysis* 21 (1961), 68–72.

NERLICH, G. C. 'Review of Stenius.' *Philosophical Books* 1 (1960), 13–16.

—. 'Review of Maslow.' *Ibid.* 3 (1962), 10–11.

—. 'If You Can't Be Wrong, then You Can't Be Right.' *Philosophical Quarterly* 17 (1967), 300–7.

NEWMAN, J. R. 'Review of *Blue and Brown Books* and Malcolm's *Memoir*.' *Scientific American* 201 (August 1959), 149–58.

NIELSEN, H. A. 'Review of Charlesworth.' *New Scholasticism* 34 (1960), 262–5.

—. 'Wittgenstein on Language.' *Philosophical Studies* (Irish) 8, (1958), 115–21.

NIELSEN, KAI. 'Wittgensteinian Fideism.' *Philosophy* 42, (1967), 191–209. See Hudson.

—. 'God and Forms of Life.' *Indian Philosophical Review*, forthcoming.

NOLET DE BRAUWERE, Y. 'Coups de sonde dans la philosophie anglaise contemporaine.' *Revue Philosophique de Louvain* 58 (1960), 250–68.

NORTHROP, F. S. C. 'Language, Mysticism and God', in his *Man, Nature and God* (New York: Simon & Schuster, 1962), 238–45.

NYGREN, ANDERS. 'From Atomism to Contexts of Meaning in Philosophy', in *Philosophical Essays Dedicated to Gunnar Aspelin* (Lund: GWK Gleerup bokförlag. 1963), 122–36.

O'BRIEN, GEORGE. 'The Unity of Wittgenstein's Thought.' *International Philosophical Quarterly* 6 (1966), 45–70; reprinted in Fann.

OLSCAMP, PAUL J. 'Wittgenstein's Refutation of Skepticism.' *Philo. and Pheno. Research* 26 (1965), 239–47.

ORR, S. S. 'Some Reflections on the Cambridge Approach to Philosophy', *Australasian Journal of Psychology and Philosophy* 4 (1946), 34–76; 120–67.

O'SHOUGHNESSY, EDNA. 'The Picture Theory of Meaning.' *Mind* 62 (1953), 181–201; reprinted in Copi and Beard.

PACI, E. 'Negativita e positivita di Wittgenstein.' *Aut Aut*, No. 9 (Maggio, 1952), 252–6.

PACIFICO. 'Il Libro Blu' and 'Il Libro Marrone', in *Dizionario Letterario delle Opere di Tutti i Tempi e di Tutte le Letterature*. Appendice, Vol. 1 (Milano: Bompiani Editrice, 1964).

PAGEE, SAMUEL. 'Of Words and Tools.' *Inquiry* 10 (1967), 181–95.

PALMER, H. 'The Other Logical Constant.' *Mind* 68 (1958), 50–9.

PASSMORE, JOHN. 'Some Cambridge Philosophers; and Wittgenstein's *Tractatus*', and 'Wittgenstein and Ordinary Language Philosophy', in his *Hundred Years of Philosophy* (New York: Basic Books Inc., 2nd revised edition, 1966), 348–68 and 431–75.

PAUL, G. A. 'Wittgenstein', in A. J. Ayer, etc. (eds.): *The Revolution in Philosophy* (London: Macmillan, 1956), 88–96. Reprinted in Fann.

PAUL, ROBERT. "B's Perplexity.' *Analysis* 25 (1966), 176–8.

PEARS, D. F. 'Logical Atomism: Russell and Wittgenstein', in A. J. Ayer, etc. (eds.): *The Revolution in Philosophy*, 44–55.

—. 'Wittgenstein and Austin', in B. Williams and A. Montefiore (eds.): *British Analytical Philosophy* (London: Routledge & Kegan Paul, 1966), 17–39.

PEDUZZI, O. 'Wittgenstein in Inghilterra.' *Aut Aut*, No. 19 (Maggio, 1954), 46–9.

PERKINS, MORELAND. 'Two Arguments Against a Private Language.' *Journal of Philosophy* 62 (1965), 443–58; reprinted in Morick.

PETERSON, R. G. 'Picture is a Fact: Wittgenstein and *The Naked Lunch*.' *20th Century Literature* 12 (1966), 78–86. (Compares the *Tractatus* to William Burrough's book.)

VAN PEURSEN, C. A. 'E. Husserl and L. Wittgenstein.' *Philos. and Pheno. Research* 20 (1959), 181–95.

PITCHER, GEORGE. 'Wittgenstein, Nonsense, and Lewis Carroll.' *Massachusetts Reviews* 6 (1965), 591–611; reprinted in Fann.

PLOCHMANN, G. K. 'Mathematics in Wittgenstein's *Tractatus*.' *Philosophia Mathematica* 2 (1965), 1–12.

—. 'A Note on Harrison's Notes on "Das Mystische".' *Southern Journal of Philosophy* 2 (1964), 130–2.

—. 'Review of Anscombe.' *Modern Schoolman* 37 (1960), 242–6.

—. 'Review of the new translation of *Tractatus*.' *Ibid.* 40 (1962), 65–7.

—. 'The Method of the *Tractatus*.' Unpublished.

—. 'Wittgenstein's Ladder.' Unpublished.

POLE, DAVID. 'Review of *Blue and Brown Books*.' *Philosophy* 34 (1959), 367–8.

—. 'Wittgenstein et la philosophie.' *Archives de Philosophie* 24, Nos. 3, 4 (1961), 450–67.

—. 'Cook on Wittgenstein's Account of Privacy.' *Philosophy* 42 (1967), 277–9.

POMPA, L. 'Family Resemblance.' *Philosophical Quarterly* 17 (1967), 63–9. See Huby.

—. 'Family Resemblance: A Reply.' *Ibid.* 18 (1968), 347–53. A reply to Huby and Llewellyn.

POPPER, KARL. 'The Nature of Philosophical Problems and Their Roots in Science.' *British Journal for the Philosophy of Science* 3 (1952), 124–56.

PRETI, G. 'Realismo Ontologico e Senso Comune.' *Rivista Critica di Storia della Filosofia* 8 (1953), 533–44. A section on the *Tractatus*.

PREUS, R. D. 'Review of *Notebooks*.' *Concordia Theological Monthly* 33 (1962), 120.

PROCTOR, G. L. 'Scientific Laws, Scientific Objects, and the *Tractatus*.' *British Journal for the Philosophy of Science* 10 (1959), 177–93; reprinted in Copi and Beard.

PULIGANDLA, R. 'The Problem of Private Languages.' *Philosophical Quarterly* (India) 39 (1966), 1–18.

PUTNAM, H. 'Dreaming and "Depth-Grammar",' in R. J. Butler (ed.): *Analytical Philosophy* (Oxford: Basil Blackwell, 1962), 211–35.

QUINTON, A. M. 'Contemporary British Philosophy', in D. J. O'Connor (ed.): *A Critical History of Western Philosophy* (New York: Free Press, 1964), 530–56; a selection from it reprinted in Pitcher.

—. 'Linguistic Analysis', in R. Klibansky (ed.): *Philosophy in the Mid-Century* (Firenze: La Nouva Italia Editrice, 1961), Vol. II, 146–202.

RADER, M. M. 'Games and Definitions; Excerpt from *Philosophical Investigations*' in his *A Modern Book of Esthetics*, 3rd edition (New York: Holt, Rinehart & Winston, 1960), 195–9.

RAJAN, R. SANDARA. 'Cassirer and Wittgenstein.' *International Philosophical Quarterly* 7 (1967), 591–610.

RAMSEY, FRANK. 'Critical Notice of the *Tractatus*.' *Mind* 32 (1923), 465–78; reprinted in his *Foundations of Mathematics* (London: Routledge & Kegan Paul, 1931); and in Copi and Beard.

RANKIN, K. W. 'Wittgenstein on Meaning, Understanding, and Intending.' *American Philosophical Quarterly* 3 (1966), 1–13.

—. 'The Role of Imagination, Rule-operations, and Atmosphere in Wittgenstein's Language-games.' *Inquiry* 10 (1967), 279–91.

RESCHER, NICHOLAS. 'Review of *Tractatus*.' *Modern Schoolman* 33 (1956), 120–2.

RHEES, R. 'Can There Be a Private Language?' *Proceedings of the Aristotelian Society*, Suppl. Vol. 28 (1954), 77–94. Reprinted in C. Caton (ed.): *Philosophy and Ordinary Language* (University of Illinois Press, 1964) and in Pitcher.

—. 'Miss Anscombe on the *Tractatus*.' *Philosophical Quarterly* 10 (1960), 21–31.

—. 'Critical Notice of Cornforth's *Science Versus Idealism*.' *Mind* 56 (1947), 374–92. (Criticizes Cornforth's criticism of the *Tractatus*).

—. 'Preface to *Blue and Brown Books*,' in Wittgenstein: *Blue and Brown Books*, v–xiv.

—. 'George Pitcher's *The Philosophy of Wittgenstein*.' *Ratio* 8 (1966), 180–92.

—. 'Some Developments in Wittgenstein's View of Ethics.' *Philosophical Review* 74 (1965), 17–26.

—. 'The *Tractatus*: Seeds of Some Misunderstandings.' *Ibid.* 72 (1963), 213–20.

—. 'Wittgenstein's Builders.' *Proceedings of the Aristotelian Society* 60 (1959–60), 171–86; reprinted in Fann.

RICHMAN, R. J. 'Something Common.' *Journal of Philosophy* 59 (1962), 821–30.

RIVERSO, EMANUELE. 'Review of Stenius.' *Rassegna di Scienze Filosofiche* 15 (1962), 255–6.

—. 'Review of Anscombe.' *Asprenas* 8 (1961), 383.

—. 'Review of *Notebooks*.' *Rassegna di Scienze Filosofiche* 15 (1962), 252.

—. 'L'analisi del linguaggio come metodo d'indagine filosofica.' *Ibid.* 16 (1963), 23–66.

ROBINSON, GUY, 'Following and Formalization.' *Mind* 73 (1964), 46–63.

ROLLINS, C. D. 'Review of Malcolm's *Memoir*.' *Journal of Philosophy* 56 (1959), 280–3.

RORTY, R. 'Pragmatism, Categories, and Language.' *Philosophical Review* 70 (1961), 197–223. (Compares Peirce and Wittgenstein.)

ROSENBERG, JAY F. 'New Perspectives on the *Tractatus*.' *Dialogue* 4 (1966), 506–17.

—. 'Wittgenstein's Theory of Language as Picture.' *American Philosophical Quarterly* 5 (1968), 18–30.

ROUATTI, P. A. 'La Positivita del Paradasso in Wittgenstein.' *Aut Aut* No. 103 (Gennaio, 1968).

RUNES, D. D. 'Ludwig Wittgenstein (a Photograph)', in his *Pictorial History of Philosophy* (New York: Philosophical Library, 1959).

RUSSELL, BERTRAND. 'The Impact of Wittgenstein', in his *My Philosophical Development* (New York: Simon & Schuster, 1959).

—. 'Introduction to *Tractatus*', in Wittgenstein: *Tractatus Logico-Philosophicus*.

—. 'Ludwig Wittgenstein.' *Mind* 60 (1951), 297–8; reprinted in Fann.

—. 'Philosophers and Idiots.' *Listener* (Feb. 10th, 1955), 248–9. Reprinted in his *Portraits from Memory* (New York: Simon & Schuster, 1951), 23–4; and in Fann.

—. 'Russell & Wittgenstein.' Selections from his *My Philosophical Development. Encounter* (Jan. 1959), 8–9.

RUYTINX, J. 'Review of Pole.' *Revue Internationale de Philosophie* 14 (1960), 106–7.

RYLE, GILBERT. 'Ludwig Wittgenstein.' *Analysis* 12 (1951), 1–9; reprinted in Fann, and in Copi and Beard. An Italian translation appeared in *Rivista di Filosofia* 43 (1952), 186–93.

—. 'The Work of an Influential but Little-known Philosopher of Science: Ludwig Wittgenstein.' *Scientific American* 197 (Sept., 1957), 251–9.

's.' (signed by). 'A Logical Mystic.' *Nation and the Athenaeum*, 32 (1923), 657–8.

's. c.' (signed by). 'Review of Malcolm's *Memoir*.' *Methodos* 10, Nos. 37–8 (1958), 92.

SAISSELIN, R. G. 'Language Game in Limbo Concerning a Certain Ludwig Wittgenstein, Written in Ordinary Language.' *Queen's Quarterly* (Canada), 69 (Winter, 1963), 607–15.

SANCHEZ-MAZAS, M. 'La ciencia, el lenguaje y el mundo, según Wittgenstein.' *Cuadernos Hispanoamericanos* 15, No. 40 (1953), 35–44 and in *Theoria* (Madrid) 2 (1954), 127–30.

SARAN, A. K. 'A Wittgensteinian Sociology?' *Ethics* 75 (1965), 195–200.

SCHIAVANE, M. 'Il pensiero filosofico di Ludwig Wittgenstein alla luce del *Tractatus*.' *Rivista di Filosofia Neo-Scolastica* 47 (1955), 225–52.

SCHOLZ, H. 'Wittgenstein: *Philosophische Untersuchungen*.' *Philosophische Rundschau* 1 (1953), 193–7.

SCHOONBROOD, C. 'Wittgenstein's *Blue Book*—Het Keerpunt in de Analytische Filosofie.' *Bijdragen: Tijdschrift voor Filosofie en Theologie* 23 (1962), 1–11.

SCHWYZER, H. R. G. 'Wittgenstein's Picture-Theory of Language.' *Inquiry* 5 (1962), 46–64; reprinted in Copi and Beard. See Stenius.

SCRIVEN, MICHAEL. 'The Logic of Criteria.' *Journal of Philosophy* 56 (1959), 857–68.

SELLARS, WILFRID. 'Being and Being Known.' *Proceedings of the American Catholic Philosophical Association* 34 (1960), 28–49.

—. 'Naming and Saying.' *Philosophy of Science* 29 (1962), 7–26; reprinted in Copi and Beard.

—. 'Some Reflections on Language Games.' *Ibid.* 21 (1954), 204–28.

—. 'Truth and Correspondence.' *Journal of Philosophy* 59 (1962), 39–56.

SHALOM, A. 'Review of *Remarks*.' *Les Études Philosophiques* 12 (1957), 433.

—. 'Wittgenstein, le langage et la philosophie.' *Ibid.* 13 (1958), 486–94.

—. 'Review of Malcolm's *Memoir*.' *Ibid.* 14 (1959), 548.

—. 'Review of Stenius.' *Ibid.* 16 (1961), 277–8.

—. 'Y a-t-il du nouveau dans la philosophie anglaise?' *Ibid.* 11 (1956), 653–64.

—. 'A propos d'une publication recente de Wittgenstein (*Lectures and Conversations*).' *Dialogue* 4 (June 1967), 103–13.

SHAPERE, D. 'Philosophy and the Analysis of Language.' *Inquiry* 3 (1960), 29–48.

SHOEMAKER, S. 'Logical Atomism and Language.' *Analysis* 20, No. 3 (1960), 49–52.

—. 'Review of Pitcher.' *Journal of Philosophy* 63 (1966), 354–8.

SHWAYDER, D. S. '=.' *Mind* 65 (1956), 16–37.

—. 'Critical Notice of Stenius.' *Mind* 72 (1963), 275–89; excerpts in Copi and Beard

—. 'Gegenstände and Other Matters: a review discussion of James Griffin's *Wittgenstein's Logical Atomism*.' *Inquiry* 7 (1964), 387–413.

SIEGLER, F. A. 'Comments', see under Garver.

SLOMAN, AARON, 'Review of Griffin.' *Philosophical Books*, 5 (1964), 8–10.

SLUGA, H. D. 'Review of Hartnack.' *Philosophical Books* 7 (1966), 22.

—. 'Review of *Bemerkungen*.' *British Journal for Philosophy of Science* 17 (1967), 339–41.

SMART, HAROLD. 'Language-Games.' *Philosophical Quarterly* 7 (1957), 224–35.

SMILEY, P. O. 'Importance of Wittgenstein.' *Tablet* 203 (Jan. 30th, 1954), 116. See Trethowan and MacIvor.

SOKOLOWSKI, ROBERT. 'Ludwig Wittgenstein: Philosophy as Linguistic Analysis', in J. K. Ryan (ed.): *Twentieth-Century Thinkers* (New York: Abba House, 1964), 175–204.

SPECHT, E. K. 'Wittgenstein und das Problem der Aporetik.' *Kant-Studien* 57 (1966), 309–22.

STEBBING, SUSAN. 'Logical Positivism and Analysis.' *Proceedings of the British Academy* 19 (1933), 53–87.

—. 'Language and Misleading Questions.' *Erkenntnis* 8 (1939), 1–6.

STEGMÜLLER, WOLFGANG. 'Ludwig Wittgenstein als Ontologe, Isomorphietheoretiker, Transzendentalphilosoph and Konstruktivist.' Critical Study of Stenius and *Remarks*. *Philosophische Rundschau* 13, Heft 2 (1965), 116–52.

—. 'Eine Modelltheoretische Präzisierund der Wittgensteinischen Bildtheorie.' *Notre Dame Journal of Formal Logic* 7 (1966), 181–95.

STEIN, ERNST. 'Die Teufelsaustreibung aus der Sprache Ludwig Wittgenstein: dem reinen Zweifel ausgeliefert.' (A review of *Philosophische Bemerkungen* with a sketch of Wittgenstein by his friend Michael Drobil.) *Die Zeit* (March 19th, 1965), No. 11, Seite 12.

STENIUS, ERICK. 'Wittgenstein's Picture-Theory of Language: A Reply to Mr. H. R. G. Schwyzer.' *Inquiry* 6 (1963), 184–95; reprinted in Copi and Beard.

—. 'Review of Bemerkungen.' *Philosophical Quarterly* 16 (1966), 371–2.

—. 'Review of Pitcher.' *Ibid.* 16 (1966), 373–4.

—. 'Den Spåkliga Beskrivning.' *Ajatus* (Philosophical Society of Finland), 16 (1950), 69–101.

—. 'Frege, Wittgenstein och bildteorin' (unpublished).

—. 'Linguistic Structure and the Structure of Experience.' *Theoria* 20 (1954), 153–72.

—. 'Uppbyggnaden av Wittgenstein's *Tractatus Logico-Philosophicus.' Ajatus* 19 (1955), 121–38.

—. 'Miss Anscombe's Retraction.' *Analysis* 27 (1967), 86–96.

—. 'Wittgenstein "Kritik av det Rena Språket".' *Societa Scientiarum Fennica Arsbok-Vuosikirja* (Helsingfors), 38B, No. 5 (1960), 1–14.

—. Letter. *Times Lit. Suppl.* (Feb. 17th, 1961), 105. Comments on a review of his book.

—. 'Mood and Language-game.' *Synthese* 17 (1967), 254–74. See Føllesdal.

STERN, J. P. Comparing Wittgenstein and Lichtenberg in his *Lichtenberg: A Doctrine of Scattered Occasions.* Indiana University Press, 1959.

STERN, KENNETH. 'Private Language and Skepticism.' *Journal of Philosophy* 60 (1965), 745–59.

STERNFELD, ROBERT. 'Review of Black.' *Philos. and Pheno. Research,* 26 (1965), 287–90.

STIGEN, A. 'Interpretations of Wittgenstein.' *Inquiry* 5 (1962), 167–75.

STOCKER, MICHAEL A. G. 'Memory and the Private Language Argument.' *Philosophical Quarterly* 16 (1966), 47–53.

STOLPE, S. 'L. Wittgensteins vag.' *Credo* 36 (1955), 110–4.

STOLTE, DIETER. 'Logic is die Hölle—Zu Wittgensteins Schriften.' *Der Monat* 14 (1961), 66–70.

STORER, THOMAS. 'Linguistic Isomorphisms.' *Philosophy of Science* 19 (1952), 77–85.

STRAWSON, P. F. 'Critical Notice of *Philosophical Investigations.' Mind* 63 (1954), 70–99; reprinted in Pitcher, and Morick.

—. 'Review of *Blue and Brown Books* and Pole.' *Philosophical Quarterly* 10 (1960), 371–2.

—. 'Review of Riverso.' *Mind* 75 (1966), 447.

STROLL, AVRUM. 'Review of Hartnack and Favrholdt.' *Journal of the History of Philosophy* 5 (1967), 190–3.

STROUD, B. 'Wittgenstein and Logical Necessity.' *Philosophical Review* 74 (1965), 504–18; reprinted in Pitcher.

STUMPF, S. E. 'Analytic Philosophy', in his *Socrates to Sartre* (New York: McGraw-Hill 1966), 437–52.

SULLIVAN, J. P. 'In Defense of Wittgenstein.' *Texas Quarterly* 10 (Summer 1967), 60–70.

SUTER, R. 'Augustine on Time with Some Criticisms from Wittgenstein.' *Revue Internationale de Philosophie* 16 (1962), 378–94.

SWANSON, J. W. 'A Footnote to Mrs. Lazerowitz on Wittgenstein.' *Journal of Philosophy* 56 (1959), 678–9. (See Ambrose.)

SWIGGART, P. 'The Incompatibility of Colours.' *Mind* 72 (1963), 133–6. Reply to Ferré.

TANBURN, N. P. 'Private Language Again.' *Mind* 72 (1963), 88–102.

TANNER, MICHAEL. 'Wittgenstein and Aesthetics.' *Oxford Review* No. 3 (Michaelmas 1966), 14–24.

TAYLOR, P. W. 'Wittgenstein's Conception of Language', in his *Normative Discourse* (New Jersey: Prentice-Hall, 1961), 263–79.

TENNESSEN, HERMAN. 'Whereof One Has Been Silent, Thereof One May Have to Speak.' *Journal of Philosophy* 58 (1961), 263–74.

THOMSON, J. F. 'Comments', see under Castañeda.

THOMSON, J. J. 'Private Languages.' *American Philosophical Quarterly* 1 (1964), 20–31. Reprinted in S. Hampshire (ed.): *The Philosophy of Mind* (New York: Harper & Row, 1966).

THYSSEN, JOHANNES. 'Sprachregelung und Sprachspiel.' *Zeitschrift für Philosophische Forschung* 20 (1966), 3–22.

TILGMANN, B. R. 'For the Account Showing That There Is or Is Not a Significant Difference Between the Views of the Earlier and the Later Wittgenstein.' *Review of Metaphysics* 16 (1962), 380–3.

TODD, WILLIAM. 'Private Languages.' *Philosophical Quarterly* 12 (1962), 206–17.

—. 'The Theory of Meaning and Some Related Theories of the Learning of Language.' *Inquiry* 8 (1965), 355–74.

TONINI, V. 'La natura della verita: Una logica realista.' *La Nuova Critica*, 7–8 (1958–59), 79–180.

TORRETTI, ROBERTO. 'Las Investigaciones de Wittgenstein y la Posibilidad de la Filosofia.' *Dialogos* 5 (1968), 35–60.

TOULMIN, STEPHEN. 'Wittgenstein and Psycholinguistics.' Isenberg lecture delivered on Nov. 22, 1968 at Michigan State University.

TRANOY, K. 'Contemporary Philosophy: Analytic and Continental.' *Philosophy Today* 8 (Fall 1964), 155–68.

TRENTMAN, JOHN. 'A Note on *Tractatus* 4.12 and Logical Form.' *Graduate Review of Philosophy* (University of Minnesota) 4 (1962), 29–33.

TRETHOWAN, I. 'Importance of Wittgenstein.' *Tablet* 203 (Feb. 6th, 1954), 140. See Smiley.

TRINCHERO, M. 'Review of Hartnack.' *Revista di Filosofia* 55 (1964), 109–11.

—. 'Review of *Tractatus* and *Notebooks*.' *Ibid.*, 495–7.

—. 'Review of Griffin.' *Ibid.* 58 (1967), 487–91.

—. 'Review of Gargani.' *Ibid.* 59 (1968), 225–30.

—. 'Review of Engelmann.' *Ibid.*, 243–4.

(UNSIGNED) 'Review of Ogden's Translation of the *Tractatus*.' *Times Lit. Supp.* (Dec. 21st, 1922), 854. Reprinted as 'Ludwig Wittgenstein.: 1922' in *Times Lit. Supp.* (August 28th, 1953), xlviii.

(UNSIGNED). 'Notice of *Tractatus*.' *Personalist* 4 (1923), 207–8.

(UNSIGNED). 'Obituary. Dr. L. Wittgenstein.' *Times* (May 2nd, 1951).

(UNSIGNED) 'A Philosophical Vocation.' (Review of the *Investigations*.) *Times Lit. Supp.* (August 28th, 1953), xlviii–l.

(UNSIGNED) 'L. Wittgenstein: Obiter.' *Blackfriars* 33 (Feb. 1952), 87. Correction of Cranston.

(UNSIGNED). 'Meaning and Understanding.' (Review of the *Blue and Brown Books*.) *Times Lit. Supp.* (January 16th, 1959), 36.

(UNSIGNED). 'The Passionate Philosopher.' *Times Lit. Suppl.*, No. 2983 (May 1st, 1959), 249–50. See Agassi.

(UNSIGNED). 'The Limits of What Can Be Said.' *Times Lit. Suppl.* No. 3069 (December 23rd, 1960), 831.

(UNSIGNED). 'Review of *Notebooks*.' *Tablet* 215 (May 6th, 1961), 440.

(UNSIGNED). 'The Essential Nature of Propositions.' (Review of *Notebooks*.) *Times Lit. Supp.* 60 (August 11th, 1961), 528.

(UNSIGNED). 'Review of Stenius.' *Times Lit. Suppl.* (December 23rd, 1961), 831. See Letter by Stenius.

(UNSIGNED). 'Wittgenstein: *Philosophical Investigations*', in Frank N. Magill (ed.): *Masterpieces of World Philosophy in Summary Form* (New York: Harper & Brothers, 1961), 1160–6.

(UNSIGNED). 'Wittgenstein in Red.' (Review of the new English translation of *Tractatus*.) *Times Lit. Supp.* (Jan. 19th, 1962), 45.

(UNSIGNED). 'Notice of the new translation of *Tractatus*.' *Twentieth Century* 170, No. 1012 (1962), 192.

(UNSIGNED). 'Review of the *Tractatus*.' *Scientific American* 207, No. 3 (Sept., 1962), 274.

(UNSIGNED). 'Wittgenstein's Yard-stick.' (Review of *Philosophische Bemerkungen*.) *Times Lit. Suppl.*, No. 3328 (Dec. 9th, 1965), 1163.

(UNSIGNED). 'Tracking the *Tractatus*.' (Review of Hartnack.) *Times Lit. Suppl.* No. 3350 (May 12th, 1966), 410.

(UNSIGNED). 'The Language of Language.' (Review of *Lectures and Conversations.*) *Times Lit. Suppl.* No. 3375 (Nov. 3rd, 1966), 1006.

(UNSIGNED). 'Review of *Remarks.*' *Choice* 3 (Oct. 1966), 666.

(UNSIGNED). 'Review of *Lectures and Conversations.*' *Choice* 3 (Nov. 1966), 783.

(UNSIGNED). 'Review of *Zettel.*' *Yale Review* 57 (Autumn 1967), viii.

(UNSIGNED). 'Review of *Zettel.*' *Choice* 5 (March, 1968), 66.

URMSON, J. O. 'Review of the new translation of *Tractatus.*' *Mind* 72 (1963), 298–300.

—. 'Facts and Pictures of Facts', in his *Philosophical Analysis* (Oxford University Press, 1956), 54–93.

VAN DE VATE, DWIGHT. 'Other Minds and the Uses of Language.' *American Philosophical Quarterly* 3 (1966), 250–4.

VERBURG, P. A. 'Het Schaakspel-Model bij F. de Saussure en bij L. Wittgenstein.' *Vijsg. Persp. Maatsch. Wet.* 1 (1960–61), 227–34.

—. 'Het Optimum de taal bij Wittgenstein.' *Philosophia Reformata* (Kampen) 26 (1961), 161–72.

VESEY, G. N. A. 'Wittgenstein on the Myth of Mental Processes.' *Philosophical Review* 77 (1968), 350–5. (Review article on *Zettel*).

VINCENZI, C. 'Wittgenstein visto da vicino.' *Civiltà delle Macchine*, Anno XI, No. 6, II, 7–8.

VLASTOS, G. 'Review of Malcolm's *Memoir.*' *Philosophical Review* 69 (1960), 105–8.

WAISMANN, F. 'Logische Analyse de Wahrscheinlichkeits-begriffs.' *Erkenntnis* 1 (1930–1), 228–48.

—. 'Über den Begriff der Identität.' *Erkenntnis* 6 (1936), 56–64.

—. 'Was ist logische Analyse?' *Erkenntnis* 7 (1939–40), 265–89.

WALSH, W. H. 'Contemporary Anti-Metaphysics', in his *Metaphysics* (New York: Harcourt, Brace & World, Inc., 1963), 120–30.

WARNOCK, G. J. 'The Philosophy of Wittgenstein', in R. Klibansky (ed.): *Philosophy in the Mid-Century* (Firenze, Italy: La Nouva Italia Editrice, 1961), II, 203–7.

—. 'Review of *Blue and Brown Books*.' *Mind* 69 (1960), 283–4.

—. 'Wittgenstein', in his *English Philosophy Since 1900* (Oxford University Press, 1958), 62–93.

WARNOCK, MARY. 'Review of *Zettel*.' *Listener* 78 (July 13th, 1967), 55.

WASMUTH, E. 'Die Tür in Rüken; Hinweis auf Leben und Werk Wittgensteins.' *Deutsche Rundschau* 80 (Oct. 1954), 1018–23.

—. 'Das Schweigen Ludwig Wittgenstein; Über das Mystische im *Tractatus Logico-Philosophicus*.' *Wort und Wahrheit* 7 (Nov. 1952), 815–22.

—. 'L. Wittgensteins Tystnad. Om "det Mystika" i *Tractatus*.' *Credo* 36 (1955), 118–25.

WEIL, GUNTHER M. 'Esotericism and the Double Awareness.' *Inquiry* 3 (1960), 61–72. (Criticism of Horgby.)

WEILER, GERSHON. 'Review of *Bemerkungen*.' *Australasian Journal of Philosophy* 43 (1965), 412–5.

—. 'Review of the new translation of the *Tractatus*.' *Philosophical Books* 3 (1962), 25.

—. 'On Fritz Mauthner's Critique of Language.' *Mind* 67 (1958), 80–7.

—. 'Review of *Notebooks*.' *Philosophical Books* 2 (1961), 16–8.

—. 'The "World" of Actions and the "World" of Events.' *Revue Internationale de Philosophie* 18 (1964), 439–57.

—. 'Is Humpty Dumpty Vindicated?' *Inquiry* 3 (1960), 278–81.

—. 'A Note on Meaning and Use.' *Mind* 76 (1967), 424–7.

WEIN, H. 'Le monde du pensable et le langage. Quelques réflexions sur la critique linguistique Wittgensteinienne et sur ses conséquences.' *Revue de Métaphysique et de Morale* 66 (1961), 102–15.

WEINBERG, JULIUS R. 'Are There Ultimate Simples?'

Philosophy of Science 2 (1935), 387–99; reprinted in Copi and Beard.

—. 'Wittgenstein's Theory of Meaning', in his *An Examination of Logical Positivism* (London: Routledge & Kegan Paul, 1936), 31–68.

WEISSMAN, DAVID. 'The Existence of Nonintrospectable Mental States', in his *Dispositional Properties* (Carbondale: Southern Illinois University Press, 1966), 119–58.

—. 'Ontology in the *Tractatus.*' *Philosophy and Phenomenological Research* 27 (1967), 475–501.

WELLMAN, C. 'Our Criteria for Third-Person Psychological Sentences.' *Journal of Philosophy* 58 (1961), 281–93.

—. 'Wittgenstein's Conception of a Criterion.' *Philosophical Review* 71 (1962), 433–47.

—. 'Wittgenstein and the Egocentric Predicament.' *Mind* 68 (1959), 223–33.

—. 'Review of Hartnack.' *Philosophical Review* 76 (1967), 385–7.

WENNERBERG, HJALMAR. 'The Concept of Family Resemblances in Wittgenstein's Later Philosophy.' *Theoria* 33 (1967), 107–32.

WHEATLEY, J. 'Like.' *Proceedings of the Aristotelian Society* 62 (1961–62), 99–116.

WHITE, ALAN. 'Logical Atomism: Russell and Wittgenstein' and 'Wittgenstein's *Philosophical Investigations*', in his *G. E. Moore, A Critical Exposition* (Oxford: Basil Blackwell, 1958), 201–8 and 225–36.

WHITE, MORTON. 'The Uses of Language: Ludwig Wittgenstein', in his *The Age of Analysis* (New York: A Mentor Book, 1955), 225–36.

WHOLSTETTER, ALBERT. 'The Structure of the Proposition and the Fact.' *Philosophy of Science* 3 (1936), 167–84.

WIENPAHL, P. D. 'Wittgenstein and the Naming Relation.' *Inquiry* 7 (1964), 329–47.

—. 'Zen and the Work of Wittgenstein.' *Chicago Review* 12 (1958), 67–72.

WILLIAMS, C. J. F. 'The Marriage of Aquinas and Wittgenstein.' *Downside Review* 78 (1960), 203–12. See Kenny.

WILSON, C. 'Wittgenstein and Whitehead', in his *Religion and the Rebel* (Boston: Houghton Mifflin, 1957), 290–322.

WINCH, PETER. 'Nature and Convention.' *Proceedings of the Aristotelian Society* 60 (1959–60), 231–52

—. 'Understanding a Primitive Society.' *American Philosophical Quarterly*, 1 (1964), 307–24.

—. 'Rules: Wittgenstein's Analysis', and 'Some Misunderstandings of Wittgenstein', in his *The Idea of a Social Science* (London: Routledge & Kegan Paul, 1958), 24–39.

—. 'Can a Good Man Be Harmed?' *Aristotelian Society Proceedings* (1965–66), 55–70.

—. 'Wittgenstein's Treatment of the Will.' *Ratio* 10 (1968), 38–53.

WIPLINGER, FRIDOLIN. 'Ludwig Wittgenstein, Sprache und Welt in seinem Denken.' *Wort und Wahrheit* 16 (1961), 528–41.

WISAN, R. H. 'A Note on Silence.' *Journal of Philosophy* 53 (1956), 448–50.

WISDOM, J. O. 'Esotericism.' *Philosophy* 34 (1959), 338–54.

WISDOM, JOHN. 'A Feature of Wittgenstein's Technique.' *Proceedings of the Aristotelian Society*, Suppl. Vol. 35 (1961), 1–14; reprinted in his *Paradox and Discovery* (Oxford: Basil Blackwell, 1966), and in Fann.

—. 'Ludwig Wittgenstein 1934–37.' *Mind* 61 (1952), 258–60; reprinted in *Paradox and Discovery*, and in Fann.

—. 'Mace, More and Wittgenstein', in Vida Carver (ed.): *C.A. Mace, A Symposium* (London: Methuen and Penguin Books, 1962). Reprinted in *Paradox and Discovery*, 148–66.

—. 'Logical Constructions' (in five parts). *Mind* 40 (1931), 188–216, 460–75; 41 (1932), 441–64; 42 (1933), 43–66, 186–202. Some parts reprinted in Copi and Beard.

WOLGAST, E. H. 'Wittgenstein and Criteria.' *Inquiry* 7 (1964), 348–66.

WOLLHEIM, RICHARD. 'Las "Investigaciones Filosoficas" de Ludwig Wittgenstein.' *Notas Y Estudios de Filosofia* (Argentina) 5, No. 17 (1954), 31–6; also in *Theoria* (Madrid) 2, 1954.

—. 'Review of *Investigations*.' *New Statesman and Nation* 46 (July 4th, 1953), 20–1.

—. 'Wittgenstein on Art.' *New Statesman* 72 (Sept. 9th, 1966), 367–8.

WOLNIEWICZ, B. 'Ludwig Wittgenstein.' *Ruch Filozoficzy* (Toruń) 22, No. 1 (1963), 8–17.

WOLTER, ALLAN B. 'The Unspeakable Philosophy of the Later Wittgenstein.' *Proceedings of the American Catholic Philosophical Association* 34 (1960), 168–93.

WOOD, O. P. 'On Being Forced to a Conclusion.' *Proceedings of the Aristotelian Society* Supp. Vol. 35 (1961), 35–44. A reply to Bennett.

WOODS, JOHN. 'The Contradiction-Exterminator.' *Analysis* 25 (1965), 49–53.

WORKMAN, A. J. 'Review of *Investigations*.' *Personalist* 36 (1955), 292–3.

VON WRIGHT, G. H. 'Ludwig Wittgenstein, A Biographical Sketch.' *Philosophical Review* 64 (1955), 527–45; reprinted in Malcolm's *Memoir*. 1966 revised version reprinted in Fann. Finnish version first appeared in *Ajatus* 18 (1954), 4–23.

—. 'Georg Lichtenberg als Philosoph.' *Theoria* 8, No. 3 (1942), 201–17.

ZDARZIL, HERBERT. 'Die Selbstaufhebung der Philosophie. Persönlichkeit und Werk Ludwig Wittgensteins.' *Hochland* 53 (1960), 107–15.

ZEICHENKO, G. A. 'Analysis of Natural Language and Present-Day Positivism.' *Voprosy Filosofii* (1964), No. 12, 99–108. (In Russian.)

ZEMACH, EDDY. 'Material and Logical Space in Wittgenstein's *Tractatus*.' *Methodos* 16 (1964), 127–40.

—. 'Wittgenstein's Philosophy of the Mystical.' *Review of Metaphysics* 18 (1964), 39–57; reprinted in Copi and Beard.

ZIFF, PAUL. 'Comments', see under Garver.

ZUURDEEG, W. F. 'Review of *Blue and Brown Books*.' *Journal of Religion* 40 (Jan. 1960), 54–5.

SELECTED ADDENDA TO BIBLIOGRAPHY

I. WORKS BY WITTGENSTEIN

Nachlass. The originals of the Wittgenstein papers are kept in the Wren Library, Trinity College, Cambridge, England. The total material microfilmed in twenty reels is now available from Cornell University Library, Ithaca, New York. A microfilm copy can be obtained for $600 or a Xerox copy for $2300. An account of the scope and character of the *Nachlass* is given by Georg Henrik von Wright in "Special Supplement: The Wittgenstein Papers," *Philosophical Review*, 78 (1969), 483–503.

Prototractatus. Notes written in 1918, forthcoming from Basil Blackwell.

Briefe an Ludwig von Ficker. Edited by G. H. von Wright and W. Methlagl (*Brenner Studien*, 1, 1969). Salzburg: Otto Müller Verlag.

"Letters to Bertrand Russell," in *The Autobiography of Bertrand Russell*, Vol. II (1914–44), 161–70.

II. WORKS ON WITTGENSTEIN

A. Books

ANTISERI, DARIO. *Dopo Wittgenstein—Dove va la Filosofia Analitica*. Roma: Edizioni Abete, 1967.

APEL, KARL-OTTO. *Analytic Philosophy of Language and the Geisteswissenschaften*. (*Foundations of Language* Supplementary Series, Vol. 4.) Translated by Harold Holstelilie. Dordrecht: D. Reidel Publishing Co., 1960.

BORGIS, ILONA. *Index zu Wittgenstein's "Tractatus" und Wittgenstein Bibliographie*. Freiburg/München: Verlag Karl Abber, 1968.

ENGEL, S. MORRIS. *Wittgenstein's Doctrine of the Tyranny of Language: A Historical and Critical Examination*. The Hague: Martinus Nijhoff, forthcoming.

ERICKSON, STEPHEN A. *Language and Being: An Analytic Phenomenology*. New Haven, Conn.: Yale University Press, 1970.

GANGULY, SACCINDRANATH. *Wittgenstein's Tractatus: A Preliminary*. Centre of Advanced Study in Philosophy, Visra-Bharati, India, 1968.

GIEGEL, H. J. *Die Logik der Seelischen Ereignisse: Zu Theorien von Wittgenstein und Sellars*. Frankfurt: Suhrkamp Verlag, 1969.

GRANGER, G. G. *Wittgenstein*. Paris: Seghers, 1969.

— (ed.). *Wittgenstein et le Problème d'Une Philosophie de la Science*. Actes du Colloque d'Aix-en-Provence, 21–26 Juillet, 1969. Published in *Revue Internationale de Philosophie* 23, no. 88–89 (1969, fasc. 2–3).

HERMANS, WILLIAM FREDERIK. *Wittgenstein in de Mode*. (Kwadraatpamfletten, 35). Amsterdam: De Bezige Bij, 1967.

HUBBELING, H. G. *Inleiding tot het denken van Wittgenstein*. Assen/Born, 1965.

HUDSON, W. D. *Wittgensteinian Fideism* (New Studies in the Philosophy of Religion). New York: Anchor Books, forthcoming.

JONES, O. R. (ed.). *The Private Language Argument*. London: Macmillan, 1970.

JONES, W. T. *Kant to Wittgenstein and Sartre* (Vol. IV of *A History of Western Philosophy*, 2nd ed.). New York: Harcourt, Brace & World, 1969.

KEYSERLING, A. *Der Wiener Denkstil. Mach, Carnap, Wittgenstein*. Graz, 1965.

KLEMKE, E. (ed.). *Essays on Wittgenstein*. Urbana: University of Illinois Press, forthcoming.

MCGUINNESS, BRIAN. Commissioned by Duckworths to write

a critical biography of Wittgenstein. Reported in *Times* (London), March 11, 1969, p. 10.

MICHELETTI, M. *Lo Schopenhauerismo di Wittgenstein*. Bologna: Zanichelli, 1967.

NOVIELLI, VALERIA. *Wittgenstein e la Filosofia*. Bari: Adriatica Editrice, 1969.

RESCHER, NICHOLAS (ed.). *A Wittgenstein Miscellany*. Vol. 5, no. 4 of *American Philosophical Quarterly* (1968). Includes articles by Walker, Hunter, Spigelberg, Coleman, and Fogelin.

RHEES, RUSH. *Discussions of Wittgenstein*. London: Routledge & Kegan Paul; New York: Schocken, 1970.

SHIBLES, WARREN. *Wittgenstein, Language and Philosophy*. Dubuque, Iowa: Wm. C. Brown Co. Publishers, 1969.

TILLMAN, FRANK A. and STEVEN M. CAHN (ed.). *Philosophy of Art and Aesthetics: From Plato to Wittgenstein*. New York: Harper & Row, 1969.

VAN PEURSEN, C. A. *Ludwig Wittgenstein: An Introduction to His Philosophy*. Translated by Rex Ambler. London: Faber & Faber, 1969.

WEDBERG, ANDERS. *Filosofins Historia IV: Fran Bolzano till Wittgenstein*. Stockholm, 1966.

WINCH, PETER (ed.). *Studies in the Philosophy of Wittgenstein*. London: Routledge & Kegan Paul, 1969.

WUCHTERL, KURT. *Struktur und Sprachspiel bei Wittgenstein*. Frankfurt: Suhrkamp, 1969.

B. Dissertations

BELL, RICHARD H. *Theology as Grammar: Uses of Linguistic Philosophy for the Study of Theology with Special Reference to Wittgenstein*. Yale University, 1968.

BLOCKER, H. E. *An Examination of Problems Involved in the Ascription of Emotive Features to Works of Art*. University of California (Berkeley), 1966.

BOGEN, JAMES B. *Aspects of the Development of Wittgenstein's Philosophy of Language*. University of California (Berkeley), 1968.

GOFF, ROBERT A. *The Language of Method in Wittgenstein's Philosophical Investigations.* Drew University, 1967.

GRANT, BRIAN E. J. *Wittgenstein on Pain and Privacy.* University of California (Irvine), 1968.

HART, WILBUR D. *Wittgenstein, Philosophy, Logic and Mathematics.* Harvard University, 1969.

KLUGE, EIKE-HENNER. *Essay in the Metaphysics of Frege and Wittgenstein.* University of Michigan, 1968.

LEMIÈRE, ARTHUR P. *An Examination of Wittgenstein's Views on Private Language.* M.A. thesis. McGill University, 1967.

LEVIN, MICHAEL E. *Wittgenstein's Philosophy of Mathematics.* Columbia University, 1969.

ROBISON, WADE L. *The Limits of Empiricism: On the Possibility of Private Language.* University of Wisconsin, 1969.

SCHACHTER, J. P. *The Core of Wittgenstein's "Investigations": A Philosophy of Language.* Syracuse University, 1969.

SCHWYZER, H. R. G. *The Acquisition of Concepts and the Use of Language.* University of California (Berkeley), 1968.

SHERIDAN, G. R. *The Privacy of Mind: An Essay on the Logic of Psychological Statements.* University of California (Los Angeles), 1966.

SULLIVAN, THOMAS D. *The Problem of Universals in the Later Wittgenstein.* St. John's University, 1969.

WALLACE, KYLE L. *Wittgenstein's Theory of Meaning.* University of Miami, 1969.

WHITE, J. F. *Cartesian Privacy and the Problem of Other Minds.* University of Colorado, 1968.

C. Articles

ALBRECHT, E. "Zur Kritik der Auffassungen Ludwig Wittgenstein's Über das Verhältnis von Sprache, Logik und Erkenntnistheorie." *Deutsche Zeitschrift für Philosophie* 16 (1968), 813–29.

AMDUR, STEPHEN and SAMUEL A. HORINE. "An Index of Philosophically Relevant Terms in Wittgenstein's *Zettel*." *International Philosophical Quarterly* 10 (1970), 310–21.

ANTONELLI, MARIA TERESA. "Linguagem e ulterioridade em Wittgenstein." *Revista Portuguesa de Filosofia* 22 (1966), 28–48.

APEL, KARL-OTTO. "Wittgenstein und Heidegger. Die Frage nach dem Sinn vom Sein und der Sinnlosigkeitsverdacht gegen alle Metaphysik." *Philosophische Jahrbuch der Görres-Gesellschaft* 75 (1967–68), 56–94.

ARRINGTON, ROBERT L. "The Logic of Our Language." *Tulane Studies in Philosophy* 16 (1967), 1–17.

BACCA, JUAN DAVID GARCIA. "Sobre las relaciones entre la logica esquematia de Wittgenstein y la logica axiomatica de Hilbert." *Acta Cientifica Venezolana* (Caracas) 2 (1951), 56–61, 103–5, 144–7.

BEARD, ROBERT. "On the Independence of States of Affairs." *Australasian Journal of Philosophy* 47 (1969), 65–8. Response to Bunting.

BEARDSLEY, M. C. "Review of *Lectures and Conversations*." *The Journal of Aesthetics* 26 (1968), 554.

BELL, RICHARD H. "Wittgenstein and Descriptive Theology." *Religious Studies* 5, no. 1 (1969).

BLACK, MAX. "Wittgenstein's Views About Language." *Iyyn* (A Hebrew Philosophical Quarterly, Jerusalem) 17 (1966), 61–4.

BLANCHOT, MAURICE. "Le Problème de Wittgenstein." *Nouvelle Revue Française* (Paris) 11 (1963), 866–75.

BOGEN, JAMES. "Professor Black's *Companion to the Tractatus*." *Philosophical Review* 78 (1969), 374–82.

BOUVERESSE, JACQUES. "Philosophie des mathématiques et thérapeutique d'une maladie philosophique: Wittgenstein et la critique de l'apparence ontologique dans les mathématiques." *Cahiers pour l'analyse*, no. 10 (1969), 174–208.

BRÄUER, GOTTFRID. "Wege in die Sprache Wittgenstein und Hans Lipps." *Bildung* (Stuttgart) 16 (1963), 131–40.

BRODBECK, MAY. "Significato e Azione." *Rivista di Filosofia* (Milan) 54 (1963), 267–93.

BUBNER, RUDIGER. "Die Einheit in Wittgensteins Wandlungen." *Philosophische Rundschau* 15 (1968), 161–84.

BURGOS, RAFAEL. "Sobre el concepto de objeto en el *Tractatus*." *Critica* (Mexico) 2 (Sept., 1968), 71–89.

BYWATER, WILLIAM G., Jr. "Wittgenstein's Elementary Propositions." *The Personalist* 50 (1969), 360–70.

CARSE, JAMES P. "Wittgenstein's Lion and Christology." *Theology Today* 24 (1967–8), 148–59.

CHASTAING, MAXIME. "Wittgenstein et les Problèmes de la Connaissance d'Autrui." *Revue Philosophique de la France et de l'Etranger* (Paris) 85 (1960), 297–312.

COHEN, MENDEL. "Wittgenstein's Anti-Essentialism." *Australasian Journal of Philosophy* 46 (1968), 210–24.

COLEMAN, FRANCIS J. "A Critical Examination of Wittgenstein's Aesthetics." *American Philosophical Quarterly* 5 (1968), 257–66.

COPLESTON, FREDERICK C. "Wittgenstein Frente a Husserl." *Revista Portuguesa de Filosofia* (Braga), 21 (1965), 134–49.

CRISTALDI, M. "Nota sulla possibilità di un'ontologia del linquaggio in Wittgenstein e in Heidegger." *Teoresi* 22 (1967), 47–86.

CUDAHY, B. "Portrait of the Analyst as a Metaphysician, the Ontological Status of Philosophy in Wittgenstein's *Tractatus*." *Modern Schoolman* 43 (1966), 365–73.

DAUERT, DIETRICH. "Der Mystische Logistiker Wittgenstein." *Die Pforte* (Esslingen), 16, H. 132 (1966–7), 66–70.

DORFLES, GILLO. "Appunti per un'estetica Wittgensteiniana." *Rivista di Estetica* (Torino-Padova) 12 (1967), 134–50.

DRUDIS BALDRICH, RAIMUNDO. "Los escritos menores de Wittgenstein," *Aportia* 1 (1964), 61–85; "Ludwig Wittgenstein (1889–1951)," *Aporia* 2 (1966), 67–87.

DWYER, PETER J. "Thomistic First Principles and Wittgenstein's Philosophy of Language." *Philosophical Studies* (Irish) 16 (1967), 7–29.

ERICKSON, STEPHEN A. "Meaning and Language." *Man and World* 1 (1968), 563–86.

EASTMAN, WILLIAM O'REILLY. "Wittgenstein, Augustine and the Essence of Language." *Philosophical Studies* (Irish) 18 (1969), 110–18.

FAIRBANKS, M. "Wittgenstein and James." *New Schoolman* 40 (1966), 331–40.

FRAYN, MICHAEL. "Battle Against Bewitchment." *New Statesman* 78 (Aug. 22, 1969), 374–82.

FOGELIN, ROBERT J. "Wittgenstein and Intuitionism." *American Philosophical Quarterly* 5 (1968), 267–74.

GALLAGHER, M. P. "Wittgenstein's Admiration for Kierkegaard." *Month* 225, no. 1205 (1968), 43–9.

GARGANI, ALDO GIOGIO. "Ludwig Wittgenstein." *Belfagor* (Rassegradi varia Umanifa, Firenze) 20 (1965), 434–65.

GOFF, ROBERT ALLEN. "Wittgenstein's Tools and Heidegger's Implements." *Man and World* 1 (1968), 447–62.

GRANGER, G. G. "L'Argumentation du *Tractatus*: Systèmes philosophiques et métastructures," in *Hommage à H. Guéroult* (Paris, 1964), 139–54.

—. "Le problème de l'espace dans le *Tractatus*." *L'Age de la Science* I, no. 3 (1968), 181–95.

—. "Sur le concept du langage dans le *Tractatus*." *Word* 23, no. 1–2–3 (1967), 196–207.

GROSS, BARRY. "Ludwig Wittgenstein: Meaning and Reference, Sensations and Mental Acts," in his *Analytic Philosophy: A Historical Introduction* (New York: Pegasus, 1970), 141–79.

HARRIS, KARSTEN. "Two Conflicting Interpretations of Language in Wittgenstein's *Investigations*." *Kant-Studien* 59 (1968), 397–409.

—. "Wittgenstein and Heidegger: The Relationship of the Philosopher to Language." *Journal of Value Inquiry* 2 (1968), 281–91.

HARTNACK, JUSTUS. "Kant and Wittgenstein." *Kant-Studien* 60 (1969), 131–4.

HEMS, JOHN M. "Husserl and/or Wittgenstein." *International Philosophical Quarterly* 8 (1968), 547–78.

HELLER, ERICH. "Wittgenstein: Unphilosophical Considerations." *Cross Currents* 17 (1967), 317–32.

HENSCHEN-DAHLQUIST, ANN-MARI. "Review of Swedish translation of *Tractatus*." *Journal of Symbolic Logic* 29 (1964), 134 f.

HINST, P. "Die Früh- und Spätphilosophie L. Wittgensteins." *Philosophische Rundschau* 15 (1968), 51–65.

HINTIKKA, JAAKKO. "Wittgenstein on Private Language: Some Sources of Misunderstanding." *Mind* 78 (July, 1969).

—. "Language-Games for Quantifiers," in Nicholas Rescher (ed.), *Studies in Logical Theory* (*American Philosophical Quarterly* Monograph Series No. 2), 1968.

HOFSTADTER, ALBERT. "Wittgenstein's *Lectures and Conversations.*" *Journal of Value Inquiry* 3, no. 1 (1969).

HOPE, V. "The Picture Theory of Meaning in *Tractatus* as a Development of Moore's and Russell's Theories of Judgement." *Philosophy* 44 (1969), 140–8.

HUBBELING, H. G. "Wittgenstein." *Streven* 20 (1966–7), 115–24.

HUBY, PAMELA. "*Tractatus* 5.542." *Philosophy* 44 (July, 1969).

HUNTER, J. F. M. "Forms of Life in Wittgenstein's *Philosophical Investigations.*" *American Philosophical Quarterly* 5 (1968), 233–43.

JANIK, A. "Schopenhauer and the early Wittgenstein." *Philosophical Studies* (Irish), 15 (1966), 76–95.

JOHNSTONE, HENRY W., Jr. "On Wittgenstein on Death." *Proceedings of the Seventh Inter-American Congress of Philosophy* (Quebec: Les Presses de l'Université Laval, 1967), 66–71.

KAMBARTEL, FRIEDRICH. "Philosophische Perspektiven der Diskussion um die Grundlagen der Mathematik. Zu Verlauf und Konsequenzen eines Kapitels der Philosophiegeschichte." *Archiv für Geschichte der Philosophie* 45 (1963), 157–93. (Pp. 183 ff. on Wittgenstein.)

KEYT, DAVID. "Wittgenstein, the Vienna Circle, and Precise Concepts." *Proceedings of the XIV International Congress of Philosophy*, Vol. II (Vienna, 1968), 237–46.

KINEN, A. E. "Visión de Wittgenstein." *Arkhé* 3 (1966), 79–90.

KING-FARLOW, JOHN. "Wittgenstein's Primitive Languages." *Philosophical Studies* (Irish) 18 (1969), 100–110.

KLEIN, PETER D. "*The* Private Language Argument and *The* Sense-Datum Theory." *Australasian Journal of Philosophy* 47, no. 3 (1969).

KOEHLER, CONRAD J. "A Study in Wittgenstein's Theory of Meaning." *Kinesis* 1 (1968), 36–42.

KREZDOM, ANTON. "Schwierigkeiten mit Wittgenstein." *Neue Deutsche Hefte* (1966, H. 2), 48–61.

KULKARNI, N. G. "Wittgenstein's Theory of Experience." *Journal of the (Indian) Philosophical Association* 11 (Jan.–June, 1968), 27–35.

KÜNG, GUIDO. "Language Analysis and Phenomenological Analysis." *Proceedings of the XIV International Congress of Philosophy*, Vol. II (Vienna, 1968), 247–53.

KURSANOV, G. A. "On Contemporary Forms of the Correspondence Theory of Truth." *Voprosy Filosofi* (1968), no. 4. English translation in *Soviet Studies in Philosophy* 8, no. 1 (Summer, 1969), 26–44.

LAZEROWITZ, MORRIS. "Wittgenstein: Post-*Tractatus*" (trad. de Alejandro Rossi). *Diánoia* (México) 12 (1966), 200–214.

LEITNER, BERNHARD. "Wittgenstein's Architecture." *Artforum* (Feb., 1970), 59–61.

LEMBRIDIS, HELLE. "Erdachtes Gespräch mit Wittgenstein (über die Philosophie)." *Club Voltaire* (Jahrbuch für Kritische Aufklärung, München) 1 (1963), 257–70, 410.

LENK, H. "Zu Wittgenstein's Theorie der Sprachspiele." *Kant-Studien* 58 (1967), 458–80.

LEVIN, DAVID M. "More Aspects to the Concept of Aesthetic Aspects." *Journal of Philosophy* 65 (1968), 483–9.

LEVYVRAZ, JEAN PIERRE. "A propos des Objets simples dans le *Tractatus*." *Proceedings of the XIV International Congress of Philosophy*, Vol. II (Vienna, 1968), 257–62.

LOKE, DON. "Review of *Lectures and Conversations*." *London Magazine* 6 (1966), 119 f.

—. "The Private Language Argument," in his *Myself and Others* (Oxford University Press, 1968), 72–109.

LONG, PETER. "Are Predicates and Relational Expressions Incomplete?" *Philosophical Review* 78 (1969), 90–8. On *Tractatus* 3.1432.

LUCAS, J. R. "On Not Worshipping Facts." *Philosophical Quarterly* 8 (1958), 144–56.

LYN, ARDON. "Family Resemblance, Vagueness, and Change of Meaning." *Theoria* 34 (1968), 66–75. Reply to Wennerberg.

MACE, C. A. "On the Directedness of Aesthetic Response." *British Journal of Aesthetics* 8 (1968), 155–60.

MATSON, WALLACE I. "Wittgenstein's *Tractatus*" and "The Later Wittgenstein," in his *A History of Philosophy* (New York: American Book Co., 1968), 466–9 and 486–90.

MAURER, A. A. "Language and Metaphysics," in E. H. Gilson (ed.), *Recent Philosophy, Hegel to Present* (New York: Random House, 1966), 520–49.

MOLITOR, ARNULF. "Bemerkungen zu Wittgensteins posthumer Philosophie der Mathematik. *Salzburger Jahrbuch für Philosophie* 10–11 (1966–67), 35–63.

MORENO, ALBERTO. "Sistema y Silencio en el *Tractatus* de Wittgenstein." *Sapientia* 25 (1970), 11–20.

MORICK, HAROLD. "Review of *Lectures and Conversations*." *International Philosophical Quarterly* 8 (1968), 651–3.

MOSIER, RICHARD D. "Reflections on the Philosophy of Wittgenstein." *Philosophy of Education: Proceedings* 23 (1967), 121–6.

MUEHLMANN, ROBERT. "Russell and Wittgenstein on Identity." *Philosophical Quarterly* 19 (1969), 221–30.

MURPHY, JOHN. "Another Note on a Misreading of Wittgenstein." *Analysis* 29 (1968), 62–4.

NIELSEN, KAI. "Wittgensteinian Fideism Again: A Reply to Hudson." *Philosophy* 44 (1969), 63–5.

NORMAN, J. "Russell and *Tractatus* 3.1432." *Analysis* 29 (1968–69), 190–2.

OSBORNE, H. "Review of *Lectures and Conversations*." *British Journal of Aesthetics* 6 (1966), 385 f.

PATRI, A. "Wittgenstein et Bréhier." *Paru* (Monte Carlo) 10 (1955), 140–4.

PEARS, DAVID. "The Development of Wittgenstein's Philosophy." *New York Review of Books*, Jan. 16, 1969, pp. 21–30:

PLANTINGA, ALVIN. "Review of High." *Commonweal* 88 (June 21, 1968), 420 f.

PLOCHMANN, GEORGE KIMBALL. "Verdad, Tautologia y Verificacion en el *Tractatus* de Wittgenstein." *Dianoia* (University of Mexico), 1968, 122–42.

RAJAN, R. SANDARA. "Wittgenstein's Conception of Criterion." *The Journal of the Indian Academy of Philosophy* 6 (1967), 45–58.

RANKIN, K. W. "Review of Griffin's *Wittgenstein's Logical Atomism.*" *Australasian Journal of Philosophy* 42 (1964), 439–44.

RAWLINS, F. I. G. "Critique of Wittgenstein's Philosophy." *Nature* (London) 183 (1959), 494.

—. "Wittgenstein's Accomplishments." *Ibid.*, 180 (1957), 399–400.

—. "A Companion to Wittgenstein." *Ibid.*, 206 (1965), 73.

RAZ, J. "Reflections on Wittgenstein's and Cassirer's Philosophies of Language." *Iyyn* (Jerusalem) 16 (1965), 121–2.

REST, WALTER. "Über Wittgenstein's *Wörterbuch für Volksschulen.*" *Rundschau* 16 (1962), 680–6.

RICKETTS, THOMAS G. "Wittgenstein's Conception of 'Criterion'." *The Undergraduate Journal of Philosophy* (Oberlin College, Ohio), 1 (May, 1969), 30–38.

RICCŒUR, P. "Husserl and Wittgenstein on Language," in Edward N. Lee and Maurice H. Mandelbaum (eds.), *Phenomenology and Existentialism* (Johns Hopkins University Press, 1967), 207–17.

RIVERSO, EMANUELLE. "Les Analyses Semantiques des Philosophische Bemerkungen de Wittgenstein." *Revue Internationale de Philosophie* 21 (1967), 508–21.

ROCHELT, HANS. "Das Creditiv der Sprache (von der Philologie J. G. Hamanns und Wittgensteins." *Literatur und Kritik*, no. 33 (April, 1969), 169–76.

RORTY, RICHARD. "Wittgenstein, Privileged Access, and Incommunicality." *American Philosophical Quarterly* 7 (1970), 192–205.

ROSENBERG, JAY. "Intentionality and Self in the *Tractatus.*" *Nous* 2 (1968), 341–58.

ROTHENSTREICH, NATHAN. "The Thrust Against Language:

A Critical Comment on Wittgenstein's Ethics." *Journal of Value Theory* 2 (1968).

ROVATTA, PIER ALDO. "La positività del paradosso in Wittgenstein." *Aut Aut*, no. 103 (1968), 79–92.

RUSSELL, BERTRAND. *The Autobiography*, Vol. II (1914–44). An account of his friendship with Wittgenstein is contained in pp. 136–40; and his letters to and from G. E. Moore concerning Wittgenstein are included in pp. 294–301.

SANJOSÉ, ENRIQUE. "Realismo Proyectivo y Atomismo Gnoseológica." *Crisis* 12 (1965), 7–33.

SANKA, FUMIO. "On the philosophy of L. Wittgenstein— From Logism to Mysticism." *The Science of Mind*, no. 8 (March 1969), 78–84. Published in Japanese by the Dept. of Philosophy, Nihon University, Tokyo, Japan.

SCARPELLI, UBERTO. "Review of Antiseri's: *Dopo Wittgenstein*." *Revista di Filosofia* 59 (1968), 88–92.

SHALOM, A. "Wittgenstein, du langage comme image au langage comme outil." *Langages* (Paris), no. 2 (1966), 96–107.

SHERIDAN, GREGORY. "The Electroencephalogram Argument Against Incorrigibility." *American Philosophical Quarterly* 6 (1969), 62–70.

SHOEMAKER, SYDNEY. "Self-Reference and Self-Awareness." *Journal of Philosophy* 65 (1968), 555–67.

SHWAYDER, DAVID S. "Reviews of Black's *Companion to 'Tractatus'*." *Foundations of Language* 5 (1969), 289–96.

SIMON, MICHAEL. "When is Resemblance a Family Resemblance?" *Mind* 78 (1969), 408–16.

SLOVENKO, RALPH. "The Opinion Rule and Wittgenstein's *Tractatus*." *ETC* (*A Review of General Semantics*), 24 (1967), 289–303.

SPIEGELBERG, HERBERT. "The Puzzle of Wittgenstein's Phenomenology." *American Philosophical Quarterly* 5 (1968), 224–56.

STEGMÜLLER, W. "Ludwig Wittgenstein." *Philosophische Rundschau*, 13 (1965), 116–52.

STEIN, ERNST. "Der Hexenhammer der Philosophie. Spät im Jahrhundert Erschien jetzt in Deutschland die erste Werkausgabe: Ludwig Wittgenstein." *Die Zeit*, 16, H. 5 (1961), 10.

SUSZKO, R. "Ontologia w Trakfacie L. Wittgensteina." *Studia Filozoficzne* (Warszawa), 68, N. 1 (1952), 97.

—. "Ontology in the *Tractatus*." *Notre Dame Journal of Formal Logic* 9 (1968), 7–33.

TEICHMANN, JENNY. "Universals and Common Properties." *Analysis* (1969), 162–5.

THOMAS, GEORGE B. "Wittgenstein on Sensations." *Philosophical Studies* 20 (1969), 19–23.

THORNTON, M. T. "Locke's Criticism of Wittgenstein." *Philosophical Quarterly* 19 (1969), 266–71.

TOULMIN, STEPHEN. "Ludwig Wittgenstein." *Encounter* 32 (Jan., 1969), 58–71.

—. "From Logical Positivism to Conceptual History," in Stephen Barker and Peter Achinstein (eds.), *The Legacy of Logical Positivism for the Philosophy of Science*. Johns Hopkins University Press, forthcoming. (On relationship between Hertz and Wittgenstein.)

WALKER, JEREMY. "Wittgenstein's Earlier Ethics." *American Philosophical Quarterly* 5 (1968), 219–32.

WATSON, RICHARD A. "Sextus and Wittgenstein." *Southern Journal of Philosophy* 7 (1969), 229–38.

WIENPAHL, PAUL. "Wittgenstein's *Notebooks 1914–16*." *Inquiry* 12 (1969), 287–316.

WILSON, FRED. "The World and Reality in the *Tractatus*." *Southern Journal of Philosophy* 5 (1967), 253–60.

WOLNIEWICZ, B. "A Difference between Russell's and Wittgenstein's Logical Atomism." *Proceedings of the XIV International Congress of Philosophy* (Vienna, 1968), Vol. II, 263–7.

—. "A Note on Black's *Companion*." *Mind* 78 (1969), 141.

WUCHTERL, KURT. "Wittgenstein's Lehre vom Ende der Philosophie." *Pädagogische Provinz* (Frankfurt), 20 (1966), 564–70.